THE AMERICAN *St. Nick*

THE AMERICAN St. Nick

WindRiver Publishing
St. George, Utah

Queries, comments or correspondence concerning this work should be directed to the author and submitted to WindRiver Publishing at:

authors@windriverpublishing.com

Information regarding this work or other works published by WindRiver Publishing Inc., and instructions for submitting manuscripts for review for publication, can be found at:

www.windriverpublishing.com

The American St. Nick

The story of The American St. Nick is based on fact. Most of the events, people, and places portrayed in the story are factual; however, some of the people are fictitious and several of the names, events and places have been novelized to better portray the actual events.

Library of Congress Control Number: 2003108955
ISBN 1-886249-08-3

First Printing, 2003

Printed in China on acid-free paper

For those who served...

FORWARD

This is the story of an event that took place during the cold, dreary days in early December 1944 during World War II in the village of Wiltz, Luxembourg and was the beginning of a personal relationship with the people of Wiltz that has endured through 59 years.

The kindness of my GI buddies to the children of Wiltz who celebrated St. Nicolas on December 5, 1944, has been reenacted every year since the end of the war.

The people of Wiltz, and indeed of all Luxembourg have never forgotten the sacrifices of Americans to free them from tyranny.

As was said at the celebration in 1977, "If Luxembourg lived another one-thousand years, we will never forget the GI friends who shed their blood so we could live in a free Europe". That declaration and its spirit are alive today!

I extend my deep appreciation to Peter Lion for his caring rendition of this extraordinary story.

Richard W. Brookins

Richard Brookins
The American St. Nick

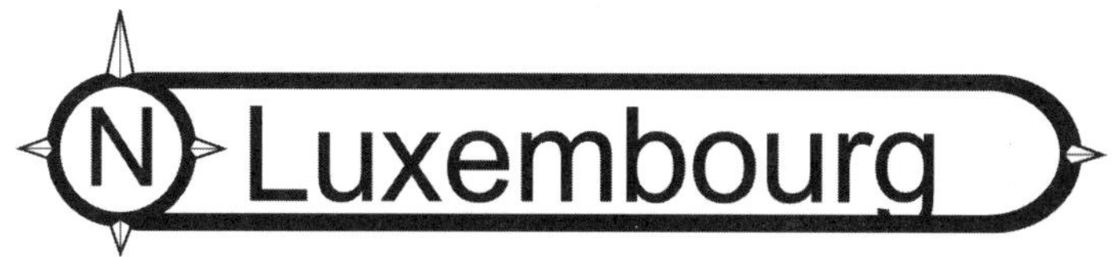

Luxembourg

©1999 maps.com
Troisvierges
Clervaux
GERMANY
50°
Wiltz
Vianden
Bettendorf
Ettelbruck
Diekirch
Rambrouch
Berg
LUXEMBOURG
Echternach
Redange
sur Attert
Mersch
Grevenmacher
BELGIUM
Mamer
Luxembourg
Hesperange
Petange
Sanem
Differdange
Bettembourg
Mondorf
Esch
Dudelange
0 5 10 mi
0 5 10 km
6°
FRANCE

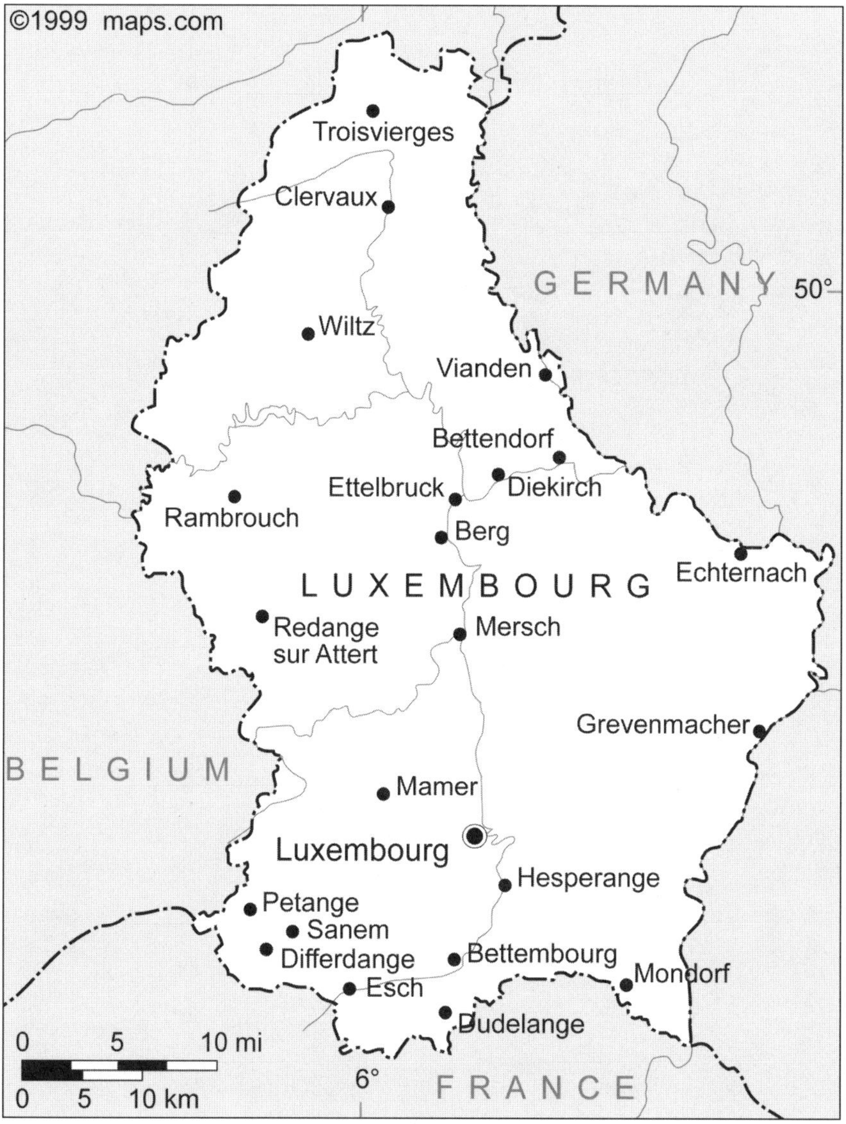

1977

A light afternoon rain fell as Frank McClelland surveyed the dense forest that surrounded him. He was surprised by how little the woods had changed. The forest floor, which saw little sunlight even on the brightest days, was still littered with pine needles, wispy ferns and the dead branches of ancient pines that stretched skyward ninety feet or more. He had come back to these woods on the outskirts of Doncols, Luxembourg, hoping to answer a question that had remained neatly folded in a corner of his mind for more than thirty years.

Frank was a solidly built man whose fifty-nine years showed in his thinning, white-streaked hair and his time-lined face. He'd always wondered what, if anything, he could have done differently back on that bitter snowy day in December 1944. It was a painful question that he had asked himself over and over through the years as time healed his physical and emotional wounds. But he knew he would never find the answer to his question without coming back to this forest and standing among these trees once again. He knew that if he could return to this wooded hillside it would somehow take him back in time, through the layers of years to December 21, 1944, when twenty-four-year-old Sergeant Frank McClelland had led his small group of MPs out of the small sleepy town of Wiltz for the last time.

The MPs had been the last of the rear guard of the American 28th Infantry Division. They had been ordered to hold the town as long as possible against the attacking Germans, buying time for the rest of the men to withdraw. Once the town was clear, Frank and his men were to move through the dense woods of the Ardennes Forest, using it for cover in an effort to elude the advancing Germans troops and get to the town of Bastogne a few miles to the west.

It was the beginning of the last major German offensive of World War II…an offensive that Army Command had deemed highly unlikely. The German army was said to be on the defensive, retreating into Germany and fortifying its defenses for a final stand against an Allied push. The fall of Berlin and the end of the war were forthcoming. There was a chance that the war might even be over by Christmas.

What command hadn't told them was that Army Intelligence had information to the contrary—information asserting that the Germans were amassing troops in the Ardennes. The commanders at Division Headquarters had also ignored information from townspeople living near the front lines. Local people had been detained, questioned by the Germans, and then released. They had risked their lives to tell the Americans what they had witnessed—the build-up of German troops, armor and artillery—but the information was set aside.

It was here in the Luxembourg hills, along a front thinly protected by American troops, that the Wehrmacht had launched a surprise counterattack and pushed through the American lines in an effort to reach Antwerp, thus splitting the Allied forces. In some of the fiercest fighting of the war, the 28th Division Headquarters in Wiltz had been overrun by the German spearhead. The Battle of the Bulge had begun.

Frank and the other MPs, along with a handful of infantry soldiers who volunteered to stay behind, held the town until the morning of December 20. When it was finally cleared of troops and any civilians who wanted to leave with the American soldiers, Sergeant McClelland and his men assembled behind a light armor tank and followed it out of Wiltz ahead of the Germans.

They had gone only about a mile toward Bastogne when they were spotted by a group of advancing German infantry. The Germans quickly opened fire and disabled the small tank with a single 75mm rocket from a PAK-40 Anti-tank gun. Machine gun and small arms fire followed and Frank and his men were forced to scatter and retreat into the thickly wooded hills.

For the remainder of the day and into the night, the men managed to dodge German troops by moving carefully and quietly through the woods. Falling snow slowed their progress but also provided some extra cover. The following day, however, the same snow that had helped hide the MPs now caused them to walk right past a group of German soldiers. The snow had concealed the Germans so well that Frank and his men didn't see or hear them until they yelled and opened fire.

The peaceful forest suddenly erupted in an explosion of gunfire. Frank and his men instinctively dove to the ground for cover. For fifteen seconds, bullets ripped the air. Then as the shooting abruptly stopped, Frank could hear someone yelling in German. He cautiously lifted his head to see several German soldiers approaching through the smoke and trees. The Germans were yelling commands as they slowly advanced, their weapons trained on the MPs. Although he understood only a few words and phases in German, Frank knew he and his men were being told to surrender. He looked around to check on his men. Most of the eight MPs only looked scared and confused, but two of them weren't moving, the snow around them blanketed in red. Frank again looked up at the advancing Germans as they continued to shout, their weapons ready to slice into the American soldiers. Realizing the hopelessness of their situation, Frank put his head down in the snow, took a deep breath, then slowly got to his knees. He tossed his Thompson submachine gun into the snow and cautiously raised his arms, all the while holding his breath. He said nothing as he surrendered. His men looked at each other for a few moments, then reluctantly mimicked his actions.

Frank would spend the next two months as a prisoner of war. He was moved to three different POW camps in Europe, then finally to a camp in Poland. By that time, the German army was back on the defensive. Their advance through Europe had been halted by the heroics and sheer tenacity of the Allied forces. Frank's POW camp was eventually liberated by the Russian army as it advanced on the Germans from the east. For Frank the war was just about over, but in those two months as a POW and for years afterward, the question lingered—what, if anything, could he have done differently to prevent his capture and the death of two of his men?

Now, after returning to the forest, Frank realized that nothing would have changed the events of that day. He and his men had been unlucky, plain and simple. Despite all their training and caution, the woods had been too thick, the snow too heavy, and the Germans too well concealed. There was no way he or his men could have avoided them.

After more than thirty years, Frank finally had his answer.

"It's a wonder we made it this far," he mumbled. "It's amazing that we all weren't killed that day."

Frank stood with his hands in his jacket pockets, took a deep breath and slowly, deliberately, gave the wooded hillside a final look. As he peered through the trees, he could feel his eyes begin to swell with tears. He looked down for a few moments and thought about the war and in particular, the friends who never made it out of these woods. He took another deep breath, cleared his throat, and turned back towards the car.

The rain was falling a bit harder and Frank thought it best to find a hotel for the night. He didn't have a planned itinerary, but he knew where he wanted to go and what he wanted to see while retracing his steps from three decades ago. Eventually, he would have to drive to the airport in Frankfort for the trip home, but for now, he had the entire week to relive the war, and that was fine with him. Tomorrow he would drive into Germany, to the site of the first camp where he had been held prisoner. But tonight he'd head to Wiltz. As far as he was concerned, his POW ordeal had begun there when he and his men were ordered to hold the town. Besides, Wiltz was the closest town where he knew he'd be able to find a hotel.

He quickly hiked the few hundred yards back to the logging road, one of many that now weaved through the forest. As he left the tree line he spotted his navy-blue rental car parked along the edge of the road, just as he'd left it hours earlier. He angled himself into the small European car, then chuckled at his absent-mindedness. He'd left the keys dangling from the ignition on the dashboard, but at least he hadn't locked himself out of the car. He started the engine, carefully maneuvered the car around on the dirt road, and headed east towards Wiltz.

The storybook town of Wiltz is a picturesque vacation retreat nestled in the forested hills of northern Luxembourg. Most of the town had been destroyed by friendly fire when the Americans were forced to retake it from the Germans during the Battle of the Bulge, but under the Marshall Plan, the town had eventually been rebuilt and to Frank's astonishment, the Hotel Bellevue was still standing.

Frank remembered it well. After the Americans liberated Luxembourg, the town of Wiltz had become the headquarters for the 28th Infantry Division, and the Hotel Bellevue had been converted into the division's HQ and mess hall. Frank also remembered how the people of the town had celebrated when the

American army liberated them and how they had opened their homes to the GIs when the soldiers had been billeted in the town. But Frank also remembered the feelings of shame, guilt, and confusion when the Americans were forced to pull out of Wiltz, once again leaving the town and its people in the hands of the Germans.

Frank arrived at the Hotel Bellevue and greeted the woman behind the desk with a broad smile and a cheerful "hello," hoping that she understood English. He'd picked up a bit of German during the war, but with no opportunity to speak it since then he knew it would be choppy at best. Getting a room for the night might be difficult.

"Hello. What may I do for you," the woman asked.

A sense of relief washed over Frank. "I was hoping to get a room for the night…just one night. I'll be leaving in the morning."

The woman appeared to be in her late sixties, with a round physique and long, meticulously braided gray hair. "Just one night then?" she asked, with a hint of a British accent.

"Yes, please. Do you have any rooms available?"

"Certainly." The woman smiled as she handed Frank a registration card and then looked for a room key in the mail slots on the wall behind her.

"I was wondering…is the restaurant still open?" Frank asked, referring to the small hotel restaurant he'd noticed on the way in. "I was hoping to get something to eat. I know it's late but I've been traveling all day."

"The restaurant? Yes, certainly."

She handed him the keys to a room and pointed the way to the elevator as he picked up his suitcase.

"Room 34. Do you need help with your luggage?" she asked, although she noticed that Frank had just the one bag.

"No, no...I think I can manage." As he rode the elevator to the third floor he wondered who would have carried his bag to the room had he replied "Yes" to the woman's question.

When he got to his room, Frank threw the suitcase on the bed, unlatched it and removed a shaving kit from the neatly packed contents. *If there's one thing the army teaches you,* he thought, *it's how to pack and travel light.* He carried the shaving kit into the small bathroom, turned on the water and washed his hands. Then he repeatedly splashed the cool tap water onto his face. He dried his hands and face, and feeling refreshed, went back downstairs to the hotel dining room.

He stood in the doorway of the restaurant for a moment, surveying the room. It was indeed small. An ornate black oak bar ran along the length of the opposite wall, allowing just eight small round tables to be squeezed into the room's remaining space. Aside from two men sitting at the bar, Frank was the only person in the room. The woman from the reception desk appeared from behind a curtain and motioned to him to sit down, then brought him a menu.

"Would you like something to drink? Some wine or beer perhaps?" the woman asked, turning her shoulders slightly towards the ornately carved bar.

"I'd love a beer…one of the local beers if possible," Frank answered and then, thinking that she might not understand the word "local" he added, "I mean one that's made in town."

"Yes of course," she smiled as she turned and walked to the bar. She placed a stein under the spigot and pulled down on the tap handle to fill the large, almost oversized beer mug.

"We have some of the best beer here in Wiltz," she announced proudly as she returned and placed the brimming mug on the table.

"Is that so?"

"Yes, in fact we here in Wiltz produce one of the finest beers in all of Luxembourg."

"Really?" Frank queried. He raised the mug to his lips and sipped.

"Oh my," he said as he licked the foam from his top lip, "this is good."

The woman smiled in appreciation. She took his dinner order, smiled once again, and disappeared behind the curtain.

Frank sipped the golden beer while drinking in the details of the dining room. He remembered the room looking much different the last time he was here, but that was during the war; everything looked different then.

It wasn't long before the woman returned with a plate and some bread.

"Your dinner should be ready soon," she told Frank, and then after a slight pause she asked, "You are visiting, yes?"

"Yes…I'm traveling all over. That is, I'm here in Luxembourg today, but I'm planning to head into Germany tomorrow."

"I see," the woman said, as she smiled and nodded, "Are you English?"

"English?" Frank replied with surprise. "No I'm an American. I was here during the war."

"Oh I see. Then perhaps you were with the American 28th Army?" the woman replied, curiosity evident in her tone.

"Yes," Frank answered, this time even more surprised. "I was an MP—that's military police—with the 28th *Division."* He emphasized the word in an effort to politely correct her mistake and wondered for a moment how she knew of the 28th Division at all.

"Yes, yes. Division, of course," she smiled. "Then you were here, at the hotel before, yes? This is my hotel. My husband and I…we were here then, during the war."

Frank looked closely at the woman, trying to peel away the layered years to recall her face.

"That's right, I remember now. You are…," his voice trailed off as he peered through the veil of time, trying to remember her name.

"Reisen, Helen Reisen."

"Reisen…yes of course. How are you?" he said, finally piecing the name into his puzzled memory.

"Very good, thank you. I am sorry, I don't…"

"Frank McClelland"

"Oh yes, I remember now."

"You do?" Frank was amazed and more than a little skeptical that she had remembered him from more than thirty years earlier.

"Of course…from earlier…at the front desk," she laughed.

"Oh yes," Frank said realizing his own error.

"I am sorry but I do not remember you from the war," Helen apologized. "It was so long ago. So many soldiers…you understand."

"Yes, I do understand. I'm glad to see you're well. And the hotel, it looks wonderful. Better than the last time I saw it."

"Well I should hope so; it was quite a long time ago. We have had time to change things." She smiled jokingly and disappeared behind the curtain for a few moments before returning with a large dinner plate.

"Is there anything else you need?" she asked as she placed the plate in front of him.

"Not right now. I think I'm all set."

"Perhaps another beer?" she offered.

"Uh…sure why not." Frank poured the remainder of the beer into his mouth.

As Helen moved to the bar and began pouring another beer, Frank noticed that she was talking to the two men at the bar and nodding in Frank's direction. She returned to the table and placed the beer in front of him, at the same time removing the empty mug.

"Excuse me, but I was wondering, since you were with the 28th Division, would you mind meeting some men from Wiltz?" She pointed out the men at the bar. "They would very much like to meet you…but after you have finished eating, of course."

"I suppose not," Frank replied, "but why do they want to talk to me?"

"They always want to meet soldiers from the 28th Division."

"Sure then, why not," Frank agreed. "But why wait...I'll talk to them now if they want."

She thanked him and walked over to the men at the bar. Frank couldn't hear what they were saying, but he didn't think it mattered since they were probably speaking in their native language. After a few moments of conversation, the two men looked over at him and smiled courteously as they rose to follow Helen back to Frank's table.

"This is Mister McClelland," Helen announced to the men. She then retreated to the kitchen, leaving the three to talk.

Frank tried to stand up to greet the men but one of them motioned politely to him.

"Please, do not get up," the man said in heavily accented English as he extended his hand. He was a thin man of medium build. His black hair was speckled with gray and he looked to be about 50 years old. "My name is Karl Mueller, and this is Franz Steiger. Good evening."

"Good evening," Frank answered cheerfully.

"Helen said you were an American soldier, and you were here in Wiltz, during the war."

"Yes, that's right."

"You were with the American 28th Division?" asked Franz, a heavier and older looking man with deep-set eyes hidden behind thickly framed glasses.

"Yes. I was an MP back then. In fact, I was captured by the Germans just outside of Wiltz, near Doncols."

"Ah yes...Doncols," Franz replied, pronouncing the name correctly.

"Will you be staying here in Wiltz long?" asked Karl.

"Well…no," Frank began sheepishly, hoping not to offend the two men, "I was planning to head out tomorrow."

"I see," said Karl. "I know you must have plans, but it would be an honor if you would stop by our museum for a tour."

"Museum? I didn't know there was a museum here in town."

"Yes, it's at the castle, our museum. Franz is the…," Karl paused as he searched for the right word in English. "How do you say it…he is in charge."

"Oh…*the curator*?" Frank offered.

"Yes…that is it. Franz is the curator…of the museum."

"It is to honor the soldiers from the Battle of the Bulge who fought here, for us, during the war; in particular, the Americans of the 28th Division," Franz explained. "The museum is in the castle, the Wiltz Castle. It would be a great honor if you could stop by and see it."

Frank could see the pride the two men had for their museum and he didn't want to disappoint them. Plus they had peaked his curiosity and now he wanted to see for himself just what would be on display in a war museum in a town this small. Most of Europe was dotted with monuments and museums dedicated to the war, but this was the first time he'd ever heard of a museum devoted almost entirely to a single unit—his unit.

"Well, why not. I'd love to," he finally agreed.

"Wonderful," Karl Mueller exclaimed. "When will you be there?"

"Well, I want to head over to Germany tomorrow, but I could come by first thing in the morning, if that's all right."

"Yes, we will be there. Is ten in the morning a good time?" Franz asked.

"Sure, that'll be fine," Frank said.

Just then Helen emerged from behind the curtain. From across the room she spoke to the two men in what sounded like German, then in English she added, "That is enough. Let him eat in peace now." Karl and Franz waved off her scolds and turned back to Frank.

"Helen...she is a wonderful cook. The best in Wiltz," Karl smiled. "Enjoy your dinner. Tomorrow...we will see you at the castle...at ten." The three men shook hands and Karl and Franz retreated back to the bar.

As Frank began eating, he couldn't help thinking about the museum. The more he thought about it, the more it interested him. He knew the American army was well regarded by the people of Wiltz, and the rest of the country for that matter. This was evident from the American flag raised alongside the Luxembourg flag at the American Military Cemetery in Hamm and at other war memorials he'd visited on his way here. But a museum dedicated to the 28th; now that was intriguing. Frank smiled to himself. He was glad the men had asked him to visit the museum. It would delay his trip into Germany, but now that he knew about the museum, he wouldn't have missed it for the world.

The Castle of Wiltz was nestled majestically in the lush forest on the outskirts of town and resembled a sprawling French chateau more than a medieval European castle. Its construction first began in the 13th century, but the castle was twice destroyed by fire, once in 1388 when French invaders burned the town to the ground, and again in 1453 when Philip of Burgundy attacked the manor. Each time the castle was rebuilt, but wars, sieges, famines and plagues often delayed construction. The castle was finally completed in 1720. Then, during the French revolution, it was confiscated, declared national property and sold at public auction. It remained in private hands for more than a century until 1951 when it was bought and renovated by the Luxembourg state. During

WWII, the castle served as a convent and girls' boarding school run by the Nuns of the Christian Doctrine. Allied bombs destroyed parts of the castle in the fighting to retake Wiltz during the Battle of the Bulge. But once again, the castle was rebuilt. It now houses a retirement home as well as a museum dedicated to the Battle of Bulge, and each year it hosts the Wiltz Festival…a series of outdoor jazz concerts.

Frank checked out of the Hotel Bellevue, had a light breakfast at a café near the center of town and then drove up to the castle. The castle looked much the same as when he last saw it in 1944, although it was obvious that it had undergone some renovations, including a large amphitheater at the back. After stopping to take a few pictures of the castle and the surrounding countryside, he went inside to meet Karl and Franz as he had promised. After he greeted them, the three began to talk about the war and the town in general as they made their way through the small museum.

A series of glass cases and displays held artifacts from the war. Among them were uniforms, both German and American, various personal items donated by individual soldiers, and standard issue equipment that any soldier might have carried—mess kits, canteens, even k-rations. There were also various weapons from both armies. Guns, bullets, mortar shells, grenades and even land mines, all rendered harmless, now lay as grim reminders of the past. And there were pictures, scores and scores of pictures lining the walls.

As the men walked through the museum, Frank stopped several times, intently looking, almost staring at the relics and pictures. A flood of memories for which he was ill-prepared washed over him.

At one of the displays Frank stopped to gaze at a German machine gun.

"That's the one," he muttered, as he pointed to the weapon. "Well not *that* one, but one just like it," he corrected, realizing that the statement had confused the two men.

"That's a German MG-42 machine gun," Frank began, his eyes still trained on the weapon. "That's what we ran into the day I was captured. Do you remember last night when I said that I was captured near Doncols? Well the way I remember it, it was pretty early in the morning and it was cold. Christ it was cold, and snowing. It'd been snowing off and on for most of the night I think. Anyway, we were scattered all over the place...and we didn't know where anyone else from the division was...it was just a mess, complete chaos. Anyway my squad was moving west...trying to get to Bastogne...that was to be the rally point. We'd left Wiltz the day before, and we were going through the woods near Doncols when all of a sudden the Germans opened up on us...with this gun...or rather one just like it. It happened so fast, and yet to me it seemed like everything was in slow motion."

Frank paused for a few moments as the memories and emotions overcame him. Karl and Franz said nothing, knowing that Frank still had more to say and realizing that anything they could add at this moment might sound trite.

"I'm sorry," Frank finally said, his voice cracking slightly. "Sometimes it's not easy remembering." Karl and Franz nodded. Frank cleared his throat, took a deep breath and then continued.

"Anyway…it was a gun like this. I can still see one of my guys, Clark, clear as day. He was walking just ahead of me…maybe ten or fifteen yards or so and a little to my left, when the woods just exploded. The Germans opened up on us all at once and Clark was hit right away…in the face…it was like his head just…," Frank stopped and looked down for a moment. The memories were so clear to him now that it made him shudder. Gaining his composure, he continued with his account.

"I guess it was instinct or training, but I dove down into the snow. The funny thing is I don't even remember doing it. I just remember looking up and seeing the Germans walking towards us, pointing their guns at us and yelling. Anyway I lost Clark and another of my guys, and the rest of us were taken prisoner."

Frank was biting down on his lip as his eyes welled-up. After a few moments he looked up at Karl and Franz and smiled tightly. Then he looked back at the gun in the display case. "Anyway…this was the gun."

Karl and Franz said nothing. They had understood every word.

"Come," said Karl softly. "There are some photographs over here."

The three men walked over to a group of simple black-framed photographs neatly arranged on the wall amid time-yellowed newspaper clippings. In each of the dozen or so black and white photos, there was a common subject: a tall man with a long white beard, who appeared to be a priest on his way to church. The man was wearing white robes which trailed behind him, and on his head he wore a bishop's miter. In his left hand he carried what looked like a Shepard's staff, and walking behind him were two children, little girls, wearing white robes and what looked like angels' wings. In one picture, the three were riding in a U.S. Army Jeep. Another photo showed the man walking through the center of town with another priest along side, and in a third picture, the group appeared to be approaching a crowd of small children who had gathered with their parents. Just in front of the children, an American soldier was playing a guitar.

Frank scanned the photographs curiously for several moments.

"Do you know this man?" Karl Mueller asked, pointing to the tall man dressed in white robes.

"Who? The priest?" asked Frank.

"No, no…*this* man; *he* is a priest," Karl stressed as he pointed to one of the other men in the picture. "This man, the one in the white, do you know him?"

"You mean he's not a priest, too?"

"No, not at all" Franz said, "He is a soldier…an American soldier…like you. That is, he was from the 28th."

"A soldier?" Frank asked with disbelief. "A GI? Really? Are you're kidding me?"

"No, he is an American soldier…from the 28th Division…from the war. He is in costume in the photograph," Franz explained.

"Oh, I see," Frank said, this time studying the figures more carefully. "No, I'm sorry, but I don't recognize him. It's a bit tough, what with the costume and all."

"But he is from the 28th...and you were in the 28th as well, yes?"

Karl's tone suggested that Frank should know the man, so once again Frank squinted through his bifocals at the old, grainy photographs and tried to recognize the soldier wearing white robes.

"It's tough to say," Frank finally conceded. "With all that stuff he's got on, I really can't make out the face, and you have to remember that there were a lot of GIs in the division...somewhere in the neighborhood of six thousand."

"Well, this man is Richard Brookins. He is from Rochester in New York." Franz said, pronouncing the town as "row-shes-tay." As he spoke, he handed Frank an old copy of a *Stars & Stripes* newspaper that Frank now noticed had been tucked under his arm the whole time. There on the front page was a copy of the same photo and the headline:

Private Brookins of Rochester Plays St. Nicolas for the Children of Wiltz.

"Oh...okay," Frank said as he looked at the photo in the paper and then compared it to the one on the wall. He reread the caption above the picture, hoping the name would spark a memory.

"No, I'm sorry, I don't know him. This was such a long time ago."

"Of course, but he was in your division" Karl repeated again, then pointedly asked, "Can you help us find him?"

"Find him?" Frank exclaimed, looking up from the tattered newspaper, "You want to find him?"

"Yes. You were in the 28th. You must help us…to find him…to locate him," Karl insisted.

"But…," Frank's voice trailed off, his mind racing, "but that was more than thirty years ago. How can I find him now? He might not have even made it out of the war? Hell, he could be dead for all we know."

"When you go back to America, if he is alive, I know you will find him. Will you help us?" Karl pleaded persuasively.

"No, you don't understand…this guy might not have even survived the war," Frank repeated, overwhelmed at the idea of finding someone based on a thirty-year-old newspaper picture. "Even if he did make it…how the hell am I supposed to go about finding him?"

"If he is alive you will find him. I know you will," said Karl with an almost infectious confidence and smile. Frank stared at the picture, his thoughts churning. What if this guy was alive, how was he going to find him? Where would he even begin looking? Would this Brookins still be living in the same town after thirty years? Frank looked up at the two men.

"So why don't you guys try to find him? Can't you call the Embassy or the Army or something?"

"Yes…yes…we have tried, but they have found nothing, so we think. We have not heard from them," admitted Franz.

"Well, if the Embassy or the Army couldn't help, what makes you think I'm going to do any better? I mean I'm sure they have records at their disposal. If they couldn't dig up anything on this guy, I doubt I'll have any better luck."

"But you were in the 28th," Karl insisted. "There must be something you can do back in America."

Frank's voice was lost with his thoughts as he looked one more time at the pictures on the wall. *This will be nearly impossible,* he thought. He stood silent for a few more moments, and then after a deep breath announced, "All right, when I get back I'll try to find him, but…"

"I know you'll do it," Karl interrupted as he patted Frank on the shoulder. "I know you will find him."

Frank took a final look at each of the photographs, hoping that maybe he had overlooked some detail that would reveal more about the tall, costumed man. But there was nothing. The three men turned to leave the museum, but after only a few steps Frank abruptly stopped. He turned and glanced at the group of photos on the wall and then back at Karl and Franz with a look of confusion on his face.

"Ok…but why?"

"Why?" Karl repeated in bewilderment.

"Yes, why?" Frank quizzed. "What's the deal? What's the story with this guy?"

Franz and Karl stared at each other, each waiting for the other to answer. It wasn't that they didn't understand Frank's question, they just hadn't expected it, and they didn't know what to say. For them, finding Private Brookins seemed so logical.

"Why do we want to find him?" Franz queried, still a bit startled.

"Well, yes…I mean, why are you so interested in finding him after all this time?" Frank somehow felt that he had offended the two men, but he wasn't sure exactly how.

"Ah," Franz suddenly brightened, "because this is a special time in Wiltz. In December we will celebrate the anniversary of our town, the rebuilding of Wiltz after the war. It will be a very big celebration. That is why you must help us to find this man."

Frank nodded. "I see. So there's a celebration...an anniversary right? I get that part, but what I don't get is why you want to find *this* guy. What does he have to do with all that?"

"We need to find him," Karl smiled, "because *he* is the American Saint Nicolas."

1944

The 28th Infantry Division of the 112th Regiment was the Pennsylvania National Guard. It was known as the "Keystone Division" because of the red keystone shaped insignia the men wore on the shoulder of their uniforms. In the months following the D-Day invasion, the division had fought its way through the French countryside. Now, with Paris liberated, the Germans were on the run and the Allies were racing towards Berlin.

The Keystone Division spent a week of much needed relief billeted in Versailles, a few miles southwest of Paris. Their break ended, however, when they were called upon to help the Parisians celebrate their liberation. Military command saw the occasion as an opportunity for publicity and on August 29, 1944, they ordered the 28th, the only complete division in the vicinity, to march into Paris and join the festivities.

All along the streets crowds gathered to cheer on the American, British and French soldiers as they made their way to the City of Lights. Once in Paris, the troops paraded before the frenzied masses that had gathered to celebrate after years of Nazi occupation. While exuberant cheers rang out, Army newsreel cameras rolled, capturing the historic moment and showing the people back home the fruits of the war effort. The cameras clicked away as row after row of the Division's soldiers proudly marched through the Arc de Triomphe and down the Champs-Elysees.

In the days and weeks immediately following their march through Paris, the men of the Keystone Division were again called upon to fight the German army as it retreated out of France. September and October saw harsh town-to-town fighting, as units of the 28th pushed their way through the Belgian countryside and on into Luxembourg. The Germans were being forced back to their well-defended homeland, a line that began in the Huertgen Forest.

The Huertgen Forest covers approximately 50 miles of the German-Belgian border south of the city of Aachen, Germany. One of the stated objectives of the American troops in the Huertgen was to take control of the dams on the Roer and Urft rivers. Allied command concluded that if the Germans controlled the dams, they could flood the forest valley below and delay the Allied advance into Germany. The flooded lowlands would render any Allied tactical bridging useless, and trap any U.S. Army units that had forded the rivers. Troops cut off by the flooding could then be easily wiped out by German reserves. The Allies also concluded that taking the Huertgen Forest would deny the German army a place to assemble a force large enough to counterattack the steadily advancing Allies. What the Allied commanders didn't know (or didn't want to acknowledge) was how well the Germans were already rooted in the Huertgen.

In peaceful times, the Huertgen Forest was a dark, ominous, almost medieval place. Its densely clustered fir and hardwoods towered overhead and their thick lower branches entangled, making it nearly impossible to move through the hills without crouching close to the ground. To make matters worse, the trees always seemed to be dripping water. The Germans took advantage of these natural obstacles and the ideal defensive terrain of deep gorges, high ridges and narrow trails, by digging into the heavily wooded hillside and creating a maze of concrete bunkers and pillboxes protected by machine gun nests, mine fields and concertina wire. It was here that the Allies chose to battle the entrenched Germans, along the now famous Siegfried line.

When the American troops began their attack in the middle of September, the lattice of thick branches and the patches of fog, along with smoke from the exploding shells, made it difficult for the soldiers to see more than ten yards in any direction. Knee-deep mud, the result of more than a month of rain, sleet and snow, rendered the few roads and logging trails that snaked through the forest useless. As a result, providing armor and air support for the American soldiers was all but impossible. The soldiers also faced a near constant cascade of German artillery shells pouring down on pre-sighted positions in the forest, while heavy machine gun and rifle fire from the bunkers and pillboxes raked the young and, in most cases, inexperienced troops as they tried to advance on the German positions. The unremitting mortar and artillery fire decimated the ranks of the American troops, turning the otherwise peaceful forest into a valley of death. The water-logged forest floor was littered with helmets, boots, canteens, broken rifles and machinery, along with torn and bloodied uniforms and the mangled bodies of dead and dying soldiers, both German and American. Despite front line reports that told of little or no progress in the attack at the expense of hundreds of lives per day, Allied commanders ordered that the advance continue.

Division after division was committed to the fight, and each time the troops were torn to pieces. Replacement soldiers, some fresh off the boat from their training in England, were sent into the forest to reinforce weary front line troops. Most of the eager young soldiers were in their late teens or early twenties, and most of them never left the forest. Some were cut down within hours after arriving. Those that did survive had to cope not only with the slaughter that surrounded them, but with dysentery, near epidemic trench foot, and in some cases even walking pneumonia brought on by wet clothes, cold food, little or no sleep, and no relief.

In the first two weeks alone, the Americans lost nearly 80% of their front line troops while making only minimal gains. Despite the deplorable battle conditions, military command continued sending fresh soldiers to the front line to maintain the assault on the well-defended German positions.

In early November, it was the 28th Division's turn to join the fight. On November 2, units of the 28th launched an attack on Schmidt, a small town the Allies considered vital to securing a foothold in the Huertgen Forest. By nightfall of the next day, a battalion of the 112th Regiment had seized the town, but other battalions lagged behind in the fighting and on November 4, German tanks and infantry counterattacked the fatigued, poorly supplied American troops, forcing them to retreat from Schmidt. For the next three days, in some of the bloodiest fighting the 28th Division would see during the entire war and under the most brutal of conditions, the battle waged nonstop for control of the town of Schmidt.

Richard Brookins was a lanky, dark-haired twenty-two-year-old corporal with the 28th Division. He was assigned as a cryptographer in the Signal Corps' message center, and it was his unit's responsibility to keep the flow of communications (coded or otherwise) open throughout the war. Now, as German artillery pounded the American positions in the forested hills around Schmidt, all he could think about was keeping his arms close to his body and his back firmly pressed against the thick trunk of a pine tree. This time the Germans were using proximity fuse shells. The shells would explode in the treetops, raining hot chards of metal and large heavy pieces of splintered wood down on the soldiers below. Many soldiers in the battle of the Huertgen Forest were killed not by bullets, but by jagged falling timber that crushed or impaled. Rather than dive to the ground for cover as they had been trained to do, the GIs quickly learned that their best chance of surviving this type of artillery barrage was to plaster themselves against a tree. In doing so, the soldiers exposed only their thick steel helmets to the exploding treetops and shrapnel.

Brookins had been returning from an aid station after helping with some wounded soldiers. The men had tried to attack a German mortar position that was systematically firing on GIs who had dug into foxholes below the ridge. The German strategy was to expend one mortar round after another on an enemy position until they killed all the soldiers huddled there. They would then direct their fire at the next position and repeat the process. Aside from the loss of life, the calculated attacks had a severe demoralizing effect on the American troops who were helpless to defend themselves. Yet getting to the German mortar positions to stop the barrage was nearly impossible. To do so required crossing thirty yards of thickly mudded, densely wooded terrain: an area that had been pre-sighted by the German mortar teams, allowing them to easily and accurately fire on the advancing troops. If the Americans managed to get past those first thirty yards, they then faced an uphill attack against bunkers that had a clear field of cross fire from the moment the men left the cover of the woods. One of the wounded men was a lieutenant who had led the ill-fated assault. He had almost reached the bottom of the hill when another soldier set off a German S-mine. The S-mine was an anti-personnel mine that when triggered, launched a projectile into the air where it exploded, spraying the surrounding area with high velocity steel balls. The young soldier had been killed instantly and the lieutenant badly wounded. The rest of the men tried to continue the assault, but the well-fortified Germans quickly repelled them.

After helping at the aid station for most of the day, Brookins had made his way back to the captured pillbox that was being used as a forward command post, all the while dodging enemy fire and skirting minefields. He was almost to the command post when the Germans began another artillery attack.

Shells began exploding in the treetops, this time only about thirty yards away. To Brookins, it seemed as though the barrage was aimed specifically at him. Three more bombs exploded in the treetops. He waited a few seconds for the fallout to clear, then ran to the pillbox that was now about sixty yards ahead of him. As he ran, the sights and sounds of battle engulfed him. Machine guns, rifle fire, mortar shells, artillery shells, exploding mines, the yelling, the screaming, the dying—all echoed through the darkening forest. As Brookins dashed across the last stretch to the bunker, the chaos ringing in his ears, he realized that he could have run right over a German position and never even known it was there. The

Germans were everywhere and Brookins couldn't see them or their positions though the dense forest and the thick smoke that hung in the air like a gray curtain.

He reached the pillbox and ducked inside, pausing for a few moments to catch his breath as the concussion of the nearby shells continued. He sat down wearily in a corner of the cement bunker, the same corner that had been his home for the past few days as he encoded and decoded messages amid the fighting that raged outside. At night he would try to fight trench-foot the way many soldiers did, by removing his socks, flattening them, and placing them inside his shirt where he hoped his body heat would dry them, or at least warm them by the next day. In the meantime, he'd remove the pair of socks that he had kept against his body that day and put them on before taking his sleeping bag outside the bunker. Once outside, Brookins would crawl into a dugout beneath some logs and try to rest for a few hours.

Suddenly another shell exploded, and then another, and a third, this time right outside the pillbox. The blast shook the earth around the bunker sending debris and large, fragmented tree limbs to the ground. The pieces landed hard and then bounced off the roof of the bunker. Inside the pillbox, dust and dirt rained down from gaping cracks in the reinforced cement ceiling. Brookins instinctively huddled deeper into his corner, grabbing at the top of his helmet which he wore even in the bunker, and trying to shield his radio and decoding equipment from the dust. As everything settled, a radioman handed him the latest transmission and Brookins quickly set about decoding it.

Within moments the message the Keystone Division had been waiting for was in front of him. The 8th and 12th Infantry Divisions were gradually being deployed to relieve the troops in the Huertgen Forest. But despite the good news, Brookins and the rest of the 28th Division would spend two more agonizing weeks in battle and incur more than six thousand casualties before relief came. So devastating were their losses that from then on, the German soldiers would refer to them as the "bloody bucket division" in reference to their red keystone shoulder patches, which the Germans said resembled buckets filled with blood. Finally, in mid-November the Keystone Division was cycled out of the Huertgen battle and sent to the rear to regroup and rest. Brookins and the other members of the Division's Signal Corps were ordered to the Division Headquarters in a small, Luxembourg town in the Ardennes called Wiltz.

The town of Wiltz, along with the rest of Luxembourg, came under Nazi occupation in May of 1940. Luxembourg had remained neutral in the years preceding the war with the government insisting that it was not a member of any alliance. The country only maintained a small volunteer army for ceremonial and educational functions, so when the Germans began their assault in Western Europe, it surprised no one that Luxembourg fell in less than a day. The country was soon under martial law and the Wehrmacht poured in, using the country as a stepping-stone for its advance through Belgium and on into France. Once the Germans were in control of Western Europe, the army gave way to the Nazi party, which took control of the small country's administration.

The Nazis considered Luxembourg to be part of the Third Reich, and sought to erase all traces of its past while reeducating the population to believe they were ethnic Germans being welcomed back to the Fatherland. The name "Luxembourg" ceased to exist, and the country was instead called "Gau Moselland" meaning "the country district." Social programs were introduced to "Germanize" the population. German laws were imposed. The speaking of "Lëtzebuergesch," the native language, was outlawed. So, too, were all non-German holidays and customs. Street names, city names, and French surnames were converted to German. Official licenses and documents were printed only in German, and anyone who resisted or publicly questioned Nazi policies was harassed, beaten, and usually imprisoned and tortured by the Gestapo.

The Nazi oppression increased with the deportation of the country's small Jewish community, and by 1942 the Germans had begun conscripting any Luxembourg male over the age of seventeen into the Wehrmacht. Young men who refused to join the German army watched as their families were taken into the streets and shot.

Public strikes were organized to protest the occupation, but they quickly ended as the Gestapo rounded up the organizers and sent them off to concentration camps as slave labor. In 1943, citizens from around the country banded together in a nationwide strike, refusing to adhere to Nazi policies and dictates. The infuriated Nazis answered the protestors by rounding up as many of the strike's organizers as they could find. Most were shipped off to concentration camps where they were never heard from again, but four of the leaders, each a respected teacher in Wiltz where the strike had begun, were forced to march to the center of town where the Germans stood them against a stone wall.

The helpless teachers watched as a German officer ordered two of his men to set up a machine gun. It only took a few moments for the soldiers to level the tripod on the stone street, mount the gun, and load a ribbon of ammunition into the breach, but for the teachers who stood silent and proud, awaiting their fate, the minutes pasted like hours.

The people of Wiltz were ordered to assemble in the town square and were forced to watch as the soldiers kneeled next to the gun, one with his shoulder pressed against the wooden butt of the gun, the other ready to feed in the string of bullets. Finally the German officer barked out orders to his soldiers who leveled the barrel of the machine gun and squeezed the trigger. The gun erupted, sending bullets ripping into the teachers. Their bodies fell quickly, but the dutiful German soldier eagerly swept the barrel from left to right and back again, even as the lifeless bodies lay in a heap on the street. Only after the ribbon of ammunition was gone did the shooting finally stop.

The soldiers disassembled their gun as the officer walked from one fallen body to the next, firing a single pistol shot into each of the four teachers as the horrified townspeople watched. Satisfied with his work, the officer ordered the tattered, blood-soaked bodies to be left in the street as a warning to the rest of the town. The general strike of Wiltz was over.

In the end, such brutal treatment only succeeded

in strengthening the opposition to German rule. A network of Luxembourg resistance groups was formed, operating throughout the country to aid downed allied flyers, hide soon-to-be conscripted youths, or organize clandestine operations to harass and disrupt the German war machine. In early September 1944, after several more skirmishes with the advancing allies, the retreating Wehrmacht finally fled Luxembourg. After nearly four years of Nazi occupation, the people of Luxembourg—their spirits once again soaring—joyfully welcomed their American liberators; and soon, thousands of soldiers rotating through the country on R&R came to know Luxembourg as a paradise for war-weary troops.

What was left of the 28th Infantry Division limped into Wiltz for R&R a few days before Thanksgiving. Prior to the war, Wiltz's rich history and tranquil surroundings had made it a favorite destination for European vacationers. Now it was the perfect spot for the battered 28th Division, not just as a headquarters, but as a reserve area located far enough from the front line fighting to allow the men to forget about the war—if only for a short time.

The men of the Keystone Division took advantage of the serene surroundings to collect themselves. Their daily duties included digging foxholes or manning forward lookout posts on the outskirts of town, or off-loading supply trucks. But it was all easy duty compared to the fierce fighting of the Huertgen Forest. When they finished their assignments, the men would enjoy hot meals and showers, clean clothes, passes to Paris, and movies and letters from home.

Most of the time, Corporal Brookins' daily duty found him in front of a radio at the division's HQ in the Hotel Bellevue. When he wasn't working on encoding or decoding messages, he would help string communication cables throughout the town and surrounding countryside. He was also one of only two men in all of Luxembourg responsible for showing movies to the soldiers on R&R. Back in training, Brookins had been given the assignment of caring for an RCA 16MM Film Projector and using it to show the latest Hollywood movies. For months after landing on the beaches of Normandy he hadn't even seen a projector; now at Division HQ he was once again the movie man, traveling from town to town and company to company with his screen and projector in tow.

On Thanksgiving Day, Brookins had set up the projector in the dining hall of the Hotel Bellevue. The room had been converted into a makeshift mess hall, with the field kitchen opposite the hotel on the Grand Rue. After the men feasted on their holiday meal, Brookins planned to show a newly arrived movie entitled, "Going My Way."

He sat near his equipment at the end of a long table in the crowded mess hall, his dinner tray filled with typical Thanksgiving fare. The mood in the dining room was light. The men laughed and joked, all the while knowing how much they had to be thankful for on this particular Thanksgiving holiday.

"Brooks…hey Brooks," a voice called from the end of the food line.

Brookins looked up to see Corporal Harry Stutz calling to him. Stutz was also in the Division's signal corps, and worked along side Brookins' at the message center. He was a solidly built man of average height with black hair, a round face and an apparently perpetual smile—the kind of smile that always made him appear mischievous. In reality, he was the epitome of the eternal optimist, always finding the good in a person or situation, even though that was becoming more difficult as the war continued.

Brookins raised a forkful of mashed potatoes in a gesture of acknowledgement, and Stutz began weaving his way through the men and tables, heading towards him.

"What are you up to Brooks, mind if I sit?" Without waiting for an answer, he placed his tray down on the table and swung his leg over the bench. "Great stuff huh? It's about time we had some decent chow around here. For a while there I was thinking that maybe the cooks were really working for the Krauts. I was getting ready to shoot them myself." He paused to shove a hunk of turkey into his mouth. "So, what's the movie tonight?"

"Going My Way…it's a Bing Crosby movie. You gonna stick around to watch it?"

"Sure why not…it's not like my dance card is filled," Stutz kidded as he showered the food on his tray with salt. Brookins chuckled a bit at Stutz's joke, then smiled and nodded toward the projector.

"I think you'll like it…I've already seen it a bunch of times. It's a good movie for the holidays."

"Yeah, some holiday…being here," Stutz said solemnly, the perpetual smile fading from his face.

A conspicuous silence fell between the two men amidst the din of the mess hall. Brookins knew what Stutz meant without having to ask; surely they would rather be home with their families, not just for Thanksgiving but for the upcoming Christmas holiday as well. More importantly, they realized that they were there enjoying a holiday meal while so many others, so many brave and honor-bound friends, were still fighting in the Huertgen Forest.

Suddenly, as if waking from a quick afternoon nap, Stutz looked up at Brookins, the smile once again on his face.

"Speaking of holidays, Christmas is just around the corner."

"Yeah, I know," responded Brookins, opening the door to a conversation he knew Harry wanted to have, "about a month from today if I read my calendar right."

"You got it," Stutz began with a tone of genuine excitement. "But I'll bet you didn't know that the people here in Wiltz haven't had much of a Christmas, or anything else for that matter, since the Krauts took over. Did you know that?"

"No, I guess I never really thought about it," Brookins answered, his eyebrows raised with genuine surprise. He began to think about the war, how long it had lasted and how long the Germans had occupied Luxembourg and the rest of Europe, but then his mind quickly wandered to how long he'd been in the war and he began to think about last year's Christmas when he was stationed in England. Brookins had celebrated Christmas with the rest of the men from the 28th Division's Signal Corps Message center. The men did what they could to make it feel like a real Christmas: they got a tree and decorated it, sang Christmas carols, had a traditional

Christmas dinner, and opened the gifts and mail their families back in the States had sent. When all that was done, the men had begun drinking, not just to celebrate, but as a way of trying to forget where they were…or more exactly, where they were not—at home.

"Well, since they haven't had much to celebrate in the way of Christmas, I was thinking of throwing some sort of party. What do you think?" Stutz's question jarred Brookins from his thoughts.

Brookins raised his eyebrows again and leaned back on the bench as if a strong wind had just blown against him. He sat looking at Stutz in disbelief.

"Did I hear you right? A Christmas party?"

"Yeah, why not? What's the matter…don't you like Christmas?"

"Sure I like Christmas…who doesn't," Brookins said, "but that's not the point. In case you haven't noticed there's a war going on."

"Exactly," Stutz countered. "That's the whole reason we should throw a Christmas party…because of this whole stinkin' mess. This town could use it."

"This town? What do you mean 'this town'?"

"Well sure, the party would be for the town too. In fact it'd be mostly for the town….but for us too," explained Stutz.

"Harry, we're not even supposed to talk to these people, remember? Don't fraternize…that's the word…and now you want to throw them a Christmas party?"

"Don't fraternize," Stutz mocked. "Are you kidding me? These people aren't working for the Krauts. Christ, Brooks…they hate the Germans more than we do!"

"Is that so? How do you figure?"

"Well, I figure from talking to this guy I met in town. His name is Schneider. Martin Schneider. We got to talking one day, and he invited me over to his house for dinner. Now I go over almost every night. And get this…not only does he cure his own ham, this guy makes homemade schnapps. It's great stuff, Brooks…it'll take the chill out of you that's for sure…probably strip the paint off a tank too for that matter. You should come over and try it one of these nights."

"Harry…?" Brookins said, steering the conversation back on course.

"What? Oh about them hating the Krauts? Well…as it turns out this guy was a member of the resistance here in Luxembourg. From what he tells me, life in Wiltz with the Germans was no picnic. They had it pretty bad. In fact, he and some of the other members of the resistance arranged some sort of a strike or protest against the Nazis. I don't know the whole story…but I guess it was a countrywide thing…everyone was in on it, and it started right here in Wiltz. Anyway," Stutz continued his tone more somber, "the Krauts came down hard on the town. They lined-up a bunch of the people who they thought organized the thing and just shot them down in the street."

Brookins lowered his head shaking it from side to side. It was another account of Nazi brutality from another liberated European town. Each time Brookins heard the story it affected him; it made him wonder how the Germans could treat innocent people so cruelly.

"Well, this guy Schneider managed to escape and go into hiding," Harry continued. "He only came back when we liberated the country, so believe me, these people ain't spying for the Germans. They hate 'em."

"No kidding?" Brookins said soaking it all in with genuine interest. "So I guess you've been over at his house quite a bit."

"Yeah…like I said, just about every night. I worked it out with the cooks so I can bring him and his wife all of our leftovers and garbage."

"Our garbage?" Brookins asked hesitantly.

"Sure…oh no, not for them…the garbage is for the pigs!" Stutz stammered. "He feeds the pigs the stuff we throw out. Like I said, you should taste his ham!"

"Wait! Hold on a second…what the hell does any this have to do with you wanting to throw a Christmas party?"

"Keep your shirt on…I'm getting to that. Well, we got to talking one night and that's when I met his niece, Martha. Brooks you should have seen her…she's the cutest thing. She couldn't have been more than seven or eight years old. She'd have melted your heart. Anyway, Martin told me that here in Wiltz the people…well the kids really, haven't had much of a Christmas to celebrate in the past four or five years thanks to the Krauts. And actually, what's an even bigger holiday around here is Saint Nicolas day."

"Saint Nicolas Day?" Brookins quizzed.

"Yeah, I guess it's pretty big here. This Saint Nicolas is their version of Santa Claus. From what I gather, Christmas is a family thing where Saint

Nicolas Day is a whole, town-wide celebration. Anyway...the kids here in town haven't seen Saint Nicolas or Christmas or whatever, in almost *five* years. Hell, there're probably some kids that were so young when the Nazis took over that they don't even know who Saint Nicolas is. It's the kids I really feel sorry for," Stutz said, jabbing at his mashed potatoes with his fork. "Can you imagine? No Christmas or anything for almost five years?"

Brookins shrugged and shook his head, "No, I guess I can't."

He loaded some buttered corn onto his fork and stared at it as he thought about what Stutz had just said...an entire town, even an entire country, prohibited from celebrating their holidays, especially Christmas. It made no sense. But then this was war, Brookins thought, and in war a lot of things just didn't make sense.

"Martin said it's looking like there won't be much for them to celebrate this year either," Stutz continued. I mean, they can celebrate St. Nicolas Day and Christmas, but they don't have anything, you know...because of the war. There's nothing to give the kids...nothing." He looked away as his emotions got the better of him, but he quickly collected himself and looked back at Brookins with his familiar broad smile.

"So I was thinking that maybe *we* could throw a little party...a Christmas party...for us and them, but mostly for them. For them it'd be a Saint Nicolas party."

"It sounds good and all Harry, I just don't think the brass are gonna go along with it," Brookins said, sensing how much the idea meant to Stutz.

Stutz looked at Brookins and smiled even wider. "They already have. I spoke to Cota himself."

"You spoke to General Cota about throwing a party…a Christmas party…here in Wiltz…and he said it was ok?" Brookins gaped.

"Ok? He thought it was a great idea. He said it was just the thing this town, and the 28th needs," Stutz beamed.

"I don't believe it!" Brookins said with astonishment.

"Believe it, buddy. Hell…he's even going to write a greeting or something on the invitations."

"Invitations? You're going to pass out invitations to this thing?"

"Sure, why not? Nothing too fancy, but it has to be in English and of course their language, whatever it's called. It's not German or French…something in between I guess…Luxembourg-ese. Anyway Martin said he could translate for us…his English is pretty good. And if he can't, we can get the teachers to do it."

"Christ, I can't believe it! You got in to talk to Cota, and what did you ask him? Did you ask him about German troop movements? No. Did you ask him where we're going next? No. Did you ask him if he thinks the war will be over soon or when we're going home? No. Instead, you, Harry, ask him about a Christmas party. You're unbelievable! So…I'm guessing you've put a lot of thought into this whole thing."

"No, not really…it just sort of came to me the other day. But about the invitations Brooks…can we do that? I mean, do we have the stuff to print up some sort of invitation? And if we do, any idea on how long it would take? The reason I ask is because this Saint Nicolas Day, well it's only about ten days from now...December sixth."

Brookins thought for a minute about the equipment the message center had at its disposal. "You know, I don't think we have that kind of stuff here, but maybe they have it at Corps or somewhere like that."

"Well, if we don't have the capability, that's alright. Martin said he could get the printer in town to do it."

"I still can't believe you got Cota to give this his stamp of approval. That's pretty good, going from 'no fraternizing' straight to throwing them a party!"

"SNAFU..." Stutz declared, "Situation normal..."

"...All fouled up," Brookins cut in, finishing the sentence.

The two shared a laugh, and then Stutz glanced over at the projector.

"Hey...what did you say the name of the picture is?"

In Luxembourg the legend of the "Kleeschen," or Saint Nicolas, is a centuries old tradition. It tells of an evil butcher who killed three children, intending to turn them into sausage. But with the help of God, St. Nicolas brought the children back to life and killed the evil butcher. According to tradition, on the night of December 5, St. Nicolas and his helper "Houseker," or Black Peter, enter all the houses in town to bring the children presents. In the days preceding his visit, the children put their shoes, originally made of wood, on windowsills or by their bedroom doors. When the Kleeschen makes his rounds on the eve of Saint Nicolas Day he leaves chocolates, candy or other sweets in the shoes of children who deserve presents. Meanwhile, Houseker, dressed head to toe in coarse black garments, carries sticks to punish those children who have misbehaved throughout the year.

After talking with Martin Schneider and his little niece Martha about Christmas and St. Nicolas Day, Harry Stutz calculated that it had been almost five years since any celebration had taken place in the town, and he was determined not to let another holiday pass by unobserved.

With little effort, Stutz was able to convince General Cota, the commander of the 28th Infantry Division, that throwing a Christmas party for the people of Wiltz would not only raise the spirits of the townspeople, but following the devastating losses in the Huertgen, would also help lift the moral of the men in the division. It might even make for a good PR opportunity. Stutz suggested that one of the film crews from the 28th Division's Signal Corps could film the event, and he offered to contact the official Army newspaper, the *Stars And Stripes,* to ask that someone come to Wiltz and do a story about the party.

After getting the go-ahead from command, Corporal Stutz gathered a small group of men from the Message Center and formed a makeshift committee to handle the party plans. St. Nicolas Day was less than a week away, and there were many things that needed to be done if the party was going to take place. Stutz assigned one of the men the task of getting the invitations written and translated, and then printed by the printer in Wiltz. Several other committee members would then distribute the invitations to everyone in town. Two men were put in charge of collecting as much chocolate and candy as they could from the soldiers. The plan was to start with the men assigned to the message center, and then branch out to other soldiers in the Signal Corps. Stutz assigned the remaining committee members the task of getting together with the Division cooks and telling them of the party plans with enough lead time to bake cakes and make donuts for the party. The baked treats then needed to be taken from the field kitchen on the Grand Rue to the party, wherever that would be. The task of finding a time and place for the party Stutz took upon himself. He thought of two possible sources of assistance: the priest at the local church and the principal of the school. Stutz reasoned that in this predominately Catholic country the head of the local church, in this case Father Wolffe, could prove invaluable. Stutz also thought that since the party was intended mainly for the children, the school principal or some of the teachers might be able to help coordinate the activities.

Stutz borrowed a Jeep from the motor pool and drove to the church near the center of town. Inside he spotted Father Wolffe, a bearded, middle-aged man dressed in a black robe, sweeping the floors of the church with a broom so old its tattered bristles were worn away to a forty-five degree angle. The priest turned as he heard the heavy wooden door close behind him. Stutz waved a "hello" and began walking towards the priest. Then, suddenly embarrassed, he quickly removed the army cap he'd worn into the building.

"Hello Father," Stutz said slowly, clearly and a bit nervously not knowing if the priest spoke English. If he didn't, Stutz wasn't sure how he was going to communicate his idea for the party. He was also a bit nervous because, although he was a catholic himself, he hadn't been inside a church in many months, too many he thought, and he was beginning to feel a bit guilty in front of the priest. He was relieved to hear Father Wolffe greet him in English, albeit with a thick accent. Without thinking, Stutz extended his hand to Father Wolffe, but as he did so his mind began to race wondering if it was proper to shake hands with a priest; he suddenly wondered if he had unintentionally insulted the priest or broken some religious taboo. Stutz was again noticeably relieved when Father Wolffe took his hand. The two men exchanged introductions and Stutz asked the priest if he had a few minutes to talk. Father Wolffe smiled and nodded as he motioned to Stutz to sit down in one of the pews.

"What is it that I can do for you?" Father Wolffe asked through his thick accent.

"Well Father, I'm not exactly sure how to put this," Stutz began, but then he saw the puzzled expression on Father Wolffe's face and realized that he might be speaking too quickly. He paused for a second, feigned a cough as if clearing his throat and then continued, this time his speech more measured.

"Father, I was hoping that you could help me with an idea I had for a Christmas party…for the town."

"A Christmas party?" Father Wolffe asked as his face clouded with bewilderment.

"Yes…it's when everyone gets together to celebrate the season…Christmas," Harry shrugged matter-of-factly, explaining the concept.

"Yes of course," Father Wolffe smiled, "I know about the holiday, but what I am wondering is…why this celebration?"

"Oh," Stutz said, realizing that he'd misread the priest's expression. "Well I was speaking to Martin Schneider...do you know him?" Stutz asked and then continued without waiting for a reply. "Well, he told me about Christmas and the whole Saint Nicolas thing...and about the Germans," Stutz said, knowing that the priest would understand the reference to the Nazi occupation. "So I was thinking that maybe we could help bring back, or at least help celebrate Saint Nicolas Day."

Father Wolffe sat back in the pew as he thought for a few moments about what Corporal Stutz had just said. Once he was sure he had understood Stutz, his face began to light up with excitement at the idea. Stutz saw the priest's obvious delight and proceeded to explain the party preparations that had already been set into motion. Then, with Stutz encouraging his input, Father Wolffe suggested that the party begin in the town square, where everyone from the town could gather, and then move by procession to the Wiltz Castle. At the castle, tables could be set up for the food provided by the cooks at the 28th Division. Stutz nodded in agreement at the priest's suggestions.

Father Wolffe then volunteered more details surrounding the traditions of St. Nicolas Day. Stutz was surprised to learn that besides the legend of St. Nicolas, there was also an actual Saint Nicolas who had lived in the second century. *That* St. Nicolas, through his deeds of helping children, became the patron saint not only of children, but of sailors and robbers as well. Stutz was a bit confused by the reference to robbers, but Father Wolffe explained as best he could with his limited English, that in the days of land barons and feudal lords, a robber was a person who stole from the wealthy to provide for those in need.

Listening to Father Wolffe explain how the St. Nicolas Day celebrations had evolved throughout the years, Stutz realized more than ever that his Christmas party was becoming a celebration of their St. Nicolas Day. It was also shaping up to be the largest event the tiny town had celebrated since their liberation three months earlier.

Stutz stood up from the pew and this time shook the priest's hand without hesitation, thanking him for his help and suggestions. He walked to the front of the church, his step buoyed with excitement, and leaned into one of the heavy wooden doors to open it. He was halfway through the door and into the cold December air when he stopped abruptly and leaned back into the church, propping the door open with his foot. Smiling sheepishly at Father Wolffe who had watched him go, he dipped the first two fingers of his right hand into the small pool of holy water beside the door, crossed himself and with a final nod to the Father, left the church.

All that was left now was to settle on a time for the celebration. Stutz climbed into the Jeep and drove to the public school where he met with the principal and several other English-speaking teachers. Stutz introduced himself and explained his party plans to the teachers, who were overjoyed at the proposal. After a brief discussion in Lëtzebuergesch, the teachers suggested that the festivities begin around three o'clock in the afternoon to accommodate the school schedules, both there and at the convent. They also suggested that the party be held on the eve of St. Nicolas Day rather than on the 6th, saying that it would be more in line with tradition. Armed with the background knowledge provided by Father Wolffe, Stutz agreed with the teachers on both the time and date of the party, and told them that invitations would be forthcoming. The teacher's faces registered a look of surprise when Stutz mentioned the invitations. They again talked amongst themselves and Stutz soon realized that they were making sure they had understood him correctly. Moments later, the teacher whose English was best of the three spoke up. She began slowly, wanting to get the translation right.

"You said invitations, yes? There are to be invitations?"

"Yes, that's right. We'll hand them out as soon as we get them printed," Stutz said gesturing with his hands as if he was dealing a deck of cards.

The teachers all smiled and thanked him.

As he left the school and headed for the Jeep, he was suddenly overcome by a feeling of uneasiness. The enormity of what this Christmas party...this *St. Nicolas* party was going to mean to the town finally hit him. He turned to look back at the school, at the teachers who were still standing at the front door, and realized why the teachers had been so surprised at the mention of invitations. The people of Wiltz had been prohibited from celebrating for more than four years and now, here he was telling them that not only would there be a Saint Nicolas Day celebration, but there would even be formal invitations.

He climbed into the Jeep and sat for a few moments thinking about the party and its meaning. There was a light, cold breeze blowing through the streets, but Stutz didn't feel it. All he could feel was the knot in the pit of his stomach. He thought of the children inside. He imagined how their faces, like the face of eight-year-old Martha Schneider, would light up when they were given the candies and chocolates and whatever else could be scrounged up such on short notice. Stutz smiled to himself as the knot in his stomach faded. He waved once more to the teachers and started the Jeep.

He drove the short distance back to HQ, satisfied that the party plans were beginning to fall into place. However, based on his conversations with Father Wolffe and the teachers, there was now one more stop he needed to make. It was something that he hadn't given any prior thought to, simply because he didn't know the details of the St. Nicolas tradition. Now he realized that it was the biggest detail of them all.

He parked the Jeep in front of the Hotel and sprinted up the stairs towards the two MPs standing guard at the entrance. Stutz had gone up only a few steps when one of the double doors opened and Corporal Brookins stepped outside.

"Brooks," Stutz called excitedly, "you're just the guy I'm looking for!"

"Oh yeah? What's up Harry?"

"I just came from the school in town. I was talking with some of the teachers there about the Saint Nicolas Party."

"The what?" asked Brookins in confusion. "Oh you mean the Christmas party thing you were talking about? How's that going?"

"So far, so good. Actually that's what I wanted to talk to you about. Have you got a minute? What do you say we get some coffee?" Stutz suggested as he tugged on Brookins' coat sleeve urging him down the stairs.

"Sure why not…I could use a cup of joe."

As the two men walked around the hotel to the mess hall, Stutz searched for a way to ease into the conversation.

"Not as cold today as I thought it would be," he said.

"No…it's actually kind of nice. It sort of reminds me of the winters back home in Rochester…if it's not snowing and the sun's out, that is. The problem is, it's usually snowing."

As the two men stepped inside the mess hall, Stutz chuckled at Brookins' reminiscing; but then, with obvious purpose, he changed the subject.

"Listen Brooks, about this party…did I mentioned that I've got guys working on all the arrangements?"

Brookins nodded, but it didn't matter since Stutz wasn't looking at him and didn't wait for a response.

"Well we formed this committee you see, and the guys are working on different things for the party. Kline's going to be handling the invitations with the printer in town, which reminds me…I need to get the details to him ASAP, and Kimmelman's talking to the cooks about getting stuff made, cakes and whatnot, and Burton and Maier are going around collecting chocolate and candy from any of the guys who want to contribute," Stutz babbled, as he poured himself a cup of coffee from the large urn at the end of the chow line.

As Brookins began filling a cup for himself, Stutz took a sip of the hot black coffee and burned his lips. He tried to cool the liquid by blowing on it and between breaths said to Brookins in a tone of utter humility, "I was hoping you'd give us a hand too."

Brookins stirred some sugar into his coffee and gave it a taste. He wrapped his hands around the cup in an effort to warm them and began gently blowing on the surface of the piping hot liquid.

"Sure Harry...I'll give you a hand, no problem. I've got a bunch of candy sitting with my gear. I really don't eat it, except for the gum...but it's all yours. Take it," Brookins said matter-of-factly, though he wondered why Stutz seemed so uneasy about asking for something that simple, especially since he'd offered to help with the party a few days earlier. "Hell, take the smokes too. I don't want them either," he grinned.

The two men laughed and then Brookins added, "I'll get the stuff for you a little later."

"Thanks Brooks, that's great, and believe me, we'll take it off your hands...except for the smokes that is...but that's not what I had in mind. I was thinking you could help us out in another way," Stutz said looking Brookins directly in the eye.

"What other way?" Brookins asked skeptically, thinking that if Stutz was being this direct, whatever he wanted was going to be big.

Stutz took off his cap and scratched nervously at the top of his head while looking down towards the floor. He took a deep breath, placed his cap back on his head and looked back up at Brookins.

"We need someone to be Saint Nicolas," he finally blurted out. He watched as a look of shock seized Brookins' face.

Brookins squinted and leaned in closer to Stutz, as if he hadn't fully understood.

"Are you serious?" he asked in a soft voice, not knowing what else to say but thinking he had to say something. He knew full well that Stutz was very serious.

"Look Brooks, remember that whole Saint Nicolas tradition I told you about? Well, it turns out we need someone to play Saint Nicolas...for the kids. Come on...it'll be easy...just like playing Santa Claus."

"Look, I've never played Santa Claus, or Kris Kringle or Saint Nick or anyone else for that matter."

"Come on...it'll be a snap. All you have to do is meet the kids, shake their hands, give 'em a pinch on the cheek, a pat on the head and send them on their way. It'll be easy."

"Snap my ass! If it's going to be so easy why don't you do it?"

"Because I'm coordinating everything, making sure everything's in place and on schedule. What do you want me to do...stop everything to be Saint Nick?"

"Well then why not one of the other guys? Look...you told me at dinner the other night that this is a big thing to these people, right? No Christmas, no Saint Nicolas Day, all because of the Krauts...right? Didn't you say that?" Brookins was pleading now.

"Well...what if I screw this up? This being such a big deal around here, what if I screw it up somehow.

What if I forget to smile at some kid or something? These people will never forget it!"

"Brooks, there's nothing to screwup," Stutz stressed calmingly. "All you have to do is just meet the kids, let them see you in the costume and..."

"Costume?" Brookins voice hit a noticeably higher pitch.

"What costume? You never mentioned anything about a costume. What costume?" His brow furrowed.

"Brooks, what did you think? Saint Nicolas would be walking around town in army issues and a steel helmet? Of course there's a costume involved, which is why I need *you*," Stutz emphasized as he reached out and put his hand on Brookins' shoulder to calm him. "Look, I spoke to the local priest earlier, his name's Father Wolffe. He's going to let you wear his mass robes, and he's about your height. You're the only guy who can fit in them."

"The only guy, Harry?" Brookins knew perfectly well that there were plenty of other guys as tall as him.

"All right, all right...sure there're other guys who could fit the robes, no question. But Brooks, would I trust them to pull this off? You're right, I did say this is a big deal to these people...and it is...I'm not going to lie to you. After talking to Father Wolffe and some of the teachers at the school, I realized that it's shaping-up to be a very big deal, especially for these kids, which is why I don't trust just anyone to do this. Come on, what do you say? It's for the kids."

Now Harry was the one pleading. Brookins could see the passion and sincerity in his eyes. It was obvious that Harry Stutz had put his whole heart into this party. Brookins looked down and thought for a few moments about Christmas and about not being home; about the war and the friends that he'd lost; about everything that happened here during the Nazi occupation; and about the children of Wiltz and the little bit of joy they might get from this St. Nicolas Day celebration. Still clutching his coffee cup, Brookins wrapped his free hand around the back of his neck and squeezed it. He looked back up at Stutz and let out a sigh as he heard himself say, "Okay...Harry, what do I have to do?"

Preparations for the Christmas party were well underway and now that Harry knew the time and the place, he could concentrate on the invitations. He jotted down a few phrases on a scrap of paper, changing and rephrasing them several times until he had the wording just right. He then headed off to the home of Martin Schneider where, over several glasses of homemade schnapps, he had Martin translated the words into Lëtzebuergesch. The next day Stutz tracked down Joe Kline and handed the paper to him with instructions to have the invitations printed in both languages. Within a few hours the invitations were ready, and the assigned men distributed them throughout town just days before the celebration. The invitations read:

THE 28th SIGNAL CO
MESSAGE CENTER SECTION
Is happy to have the children of Wiltz, Luxembourg, as their guests for our Santa Claus Party
On Tuesday, December 5, 1944
In the large room of the PENSIONNAT
From 6-8 P.M.

December 5, 1944, was a cold but sunny day in Wiltz and a sense of anticipation and excitement hung in the crisp air. For the townspeople, the party meant a return to the way of life they had enjoyed before the war. They would finally be able to celebrate the holiday season freely and without fear of consequence from the Nazis, beginning, as was the tradition, with St. Nicolas day.

For the few soldiers of the 28th Division who were involved with the party, it was a chance to enjoy the spirit of Christmas, despite not being with their families. Even with the Germans on the run, the war was far from being over; the Keystone Division knew there was no way they'd be home by Christmas, and they saw the party as a chance to celebrate as best they could—while they could. After all, Christmas day was still three weeks away. No one knew if or when orders would come, sending the men to God-only-knows-where by December 25. The occasional mortar burst or artillery shell off in the distance was a harsh reminder that the war was still being fought, and not far from Wiltz. The men lived each day with the knowledge that they could be back at the front, in the thick of the fighting, at any time and that each day could be their last. It was an obvious conclusion then that this could also be their last Christmas, and they were determined to make the most of it.

It was a little past two o'clock in the afternoon when Corporal Stutz walked into Division HQ to look for Brookins. He spotted him in a small room next to the communications center cleaning the film projector. Brookins had returned to headquarters that morning after spending a night in the town of Clervaux, just to the north of Wiltz. He had shown "Going My Way" to a group of GIs from the 110th Division who had just been rotated out of the fighting that still raged in the Huertgen Forest. After the movie, Brookins and Keith Burton, a good friend from the 28th who had accompanied him, packed up the film equipment and loaded it into the Jeep. When they finished, Burton suggested that they remain in Clervaux for the night rather than risk driving back to Wiltz through the pitch-black, hilly countryside on icy roads. Brookins agreed and the two returned to Wiltz the following morning.

"Hey St. Nick, are you ready for the festivities?" Stutz called out to Brookins from across the room,

"Very funny," Brookins said acerbically, as he shot Stutz a look of mild displeasure.

"Come on…it's going to be fun. You'll see."

"Fun? I'm not sure this is exactly what I'd call fun, Harry."

"Would you rather be on KP or pulling guard duty? Look, the kids are going to love it, and that's all that matters. Are you about ready to go?"

"Go? Go where?"

"To the Castle…to get dressed. Father Wolffe and some nuns are there waiting for you. They've got his robes and stuff for you."

"Now?" Brookins asked, as he gestured to the gutted film projector sprawled out on the table in front of him.

"Well, yeah," Stutz said. He thrust his left arm out to roll up his sleeve and at the same time glanced at his watch.

"We're looking at fourteen-hundred now…by the time you get to the castle, get dressed and all, it should be pretty close to show time."

"All right. Just let me put this stuff back together and I'll head up there."

"Ok, but Burton's outside in a Jeep waiting for you…so whenever you're ready."

"Tell him to keep the engine running…I'll be out in a second."

Brookins quickly finished cleaning the sprockets of the film projector. A small rubber aspirator like those used in hospital nurseries made an ideal tool for the machine's intricate parts. When Brookins squeezed the soft rubber ball, a burst of air was forced from the narrow cone-shaped tip—gently blowing away dust and lint that found its way into the projector's interior. A soft bristle brush and a clean rag completed the tool set and allowed him to keep the projector relatively clean. Next he used a piece of linen he'd found to wipe off the glass lens. He would have preferred a piece of lens paper designed specifically for cleaning camera lenses, but there wasn't any around and he hadn't seen a packet of it—despite requisitioning some—since the trip from England. The projector was also missing its lens cover, so Brookins improvised by draping the piece of linen over the lens like a hood before closing the machine in its travel case. He placed it on the floor with the rest of his equipment, then grabbed his jacket and wool cap and hurried outside.

Brookins immediately saw Burton, sitting behind the wheel of a Jeep. Keith Burton was a man with an average build, black hair and an olive-toned round face. He was a couple of years older than Brookins, but most importantly, he was from Buffalo, New York, not far from Brookins' hometown of Rochester, *and when you're standing in the middle of nowhere,* Burton had remarked when the two first met in basic training, *that's as good as being next-door neighbors.* Burton was a relatively quiet guy, but he and Brookins would often talk about home and places they both knew and, of course, the snow.

"How's it going Keith? Looks like you're my chauffeur," Brookins said as he climbed into the jeep. "To the castle James!" he said as he waved his arm around in a circle and pointed forward with a grandiose air.

"Anything you say Nick," Burton retaliated with a laugh. He pushed down on the clutch and put the Jeep into gear.

"Remember, it's *Saint* Nick to you, pal!" Brookins countered.

"Yeah? Well I've been around you long enough to know that you ain't no saint, that's for sure!"

They both laughed as Burton released the clutch and the Jeep jerked forward. Soon they were on their way through the streets of Wiltz to the outskirts of town and the Wiltz Castle.

It was only about a ten-minute drive from the Hotel Bellevue to the Wiltz Castle. Burton drove down the long, slushy cobblestone drive leading through the main portal and into the courtyard. He parked the Jeep in front of a door that served as the entrance to the convent. As the two men got out of the Jeep, the heavy wooden door creaked open and two nuns stepped out. The nuns looked the men over for a moment and then motioned for them to come inside. The door closed behind them and Father Wolffe greeted them from the dark foyer.

"Hello, I am Father Wolffe."

"Hello Father," the men answered in unison.

"I spoke with Corporal Stutz. Which of you is to be Saint Nicolas?" the priest asked joyfully.

"That's me…I mean…I am," Brookins said.

"I see…and your name?"

"Oh, I'm sorry." Brookins removed his cap and extended his hand. "Brookins…Corporal Richard Brookins, and this is Keith Burton. He drove the Jeep." "How's it going Father," Burton said as he removed his helmet and shook the priest's hand.

"Oh, I almost forgot!" Burton turned and dashed out of the foyer, leaving Brookins and the others standing in uncomfortable silence. Brookins blew into his hands and rubbed them together to warm them as he smiled nervously at the nuns and Father Wolffe.

"A little cold today," he said, trying to think of the German word for cold. The word was on the tip of his tongue when the door to the foyer swung open, breaking the uneasy silence, and a slightly winded Keith Burton stepped into the room.

"Sorry Father…Corporal Stutz told me to give you this…for the church he said." Burton handed a new army issued broom to the priest.

Father Wolffe smiled and nodded as he accepted the gift.

"I must thank him…it is very kind," the priest said as he inspected the broom.

"What's that all about?" a confused Brookins said softly to Burton.

"I don't know. Harry just told me to make sure the priest got it. I guess he needed a broom."

Father Wolffe then spoke to the nuns in Lëtzebuergesch. The nuns smiled and bowed slightly towards Brookins and Burton. It was obvious that the two men had just been introduced, so Brookins smiled and gave a little wave towards the nuns, and Burton mimicked him.

"Well, if you are ready, the sisters and I will help you with the robes," Father Wolffe said, motioning to a room off the foyer.

"Oh sure…ready as I'll ever be."

"I'll just wait here," Burton said, smirking and pointing his thumb at one of the large, ornately carved chairs in the foyer.

"Coward," Brookins taunted, then followed Father Wolffe and the nuns into the room.

"Everything is here," Father Wolffe said as he motioned to the table in the center of the room. On the table was a long white priest's cassock trimmed in lace, an outer cape made of heavy wool and adorned with hand sewn gold stars and gold braid edging, a bishop's miter, a pair of white cloth gloves and something that looked like a pile of frayed rope.

"The sisters will help you with everything. I must tend to some things and then I will meet you when you are ready."

"Ok…thanks Father," Brookins said as the priest bowed slightly and left the room.

Brookins suddenly realized that with Father Wolffe gone, no one in the room could communicate with him. The nuns hadn't spoken and didn't seem to understand English, and he certainly didn't understand their language. However, he had managed to pick up some German since he'd been on the continent, and between that and some miming, the three were able to get him ready.

Brookins donned the priest's white cassock over his uniform. It came in two parts, both of which were made of very light linen. The first piece, worn as a foundation garment,was unremarkable, while the second robe was a bit shorter than the first and more elaborately decorated with red and gold fabric and a light lace trim in front. The nuns helped Brookins with the heavy wool outer cape, draping it over his head like a poncho. The cape was only about waist high in the front, but it was long and trailed after him in back.

Once Brookins was properly dressed, one of the nuns picked-up the pile of frayed rope and handed it to him. Brookins quickly realized that the lumpy rope was to be his "beard." *Of course,* he thought to himself, *what would Santa Claus or Saint Nick be without a white beard?* The nuns tied the rope beard in place with a ribbon. The beard hung from just beneath Brookins' nose, down to his chest, and there was a hole cut in it for his mouth.

Next came the bishop's miter. The nuns tried to place it on top of Brookins' head but it was too small and wouldn't stay. After several attempts to push the hat onto his head, Brookins took the hat from them and gently pulled at the headband, stretching it as much as he could without tearing it. Finally, after a few minutes and a few more attempts by the sisters to force the hat onto Brookins' head, the hat had stretched enough for him to wear it. It was tight, very tight, but it was as loose as it was going to get without ripping.

Brookins was just about finished when the door opened and Father Wolffe ushered in two little girls who looked to be about eight or nine years old.

"What would Saint Nicolas be without his *engel,*" the priest said, but then paused as he tried to remember the word in English. "Angel. We have angel for you. Anna and Greta Shultzmann. They are from the school here. They are sisters—the best of their class. They will be your help."

The girls wore white dresses with white socks and shoes, and attached to each of their dresses was a pair of cloth angel's wings held in place with white ribbon and tied in front with a bow. The girls also wore white ribbons around their heads meant to look like halos. Brookins smiled at them but said nothing, knowing that they wouldn't understand him anyway.

One of the nuns walked over and picked up a crozier, a sort of Shepard's staff that had been leaning against the wall, and offered it to Brookins. He quickly pulled on the white cloth gloves and took the crozier from the nun.

"Shall we go?" Father Wolffe asked.

Brookins examined the crozier for a moment then nodded to Father Wolffe. The two girls left the room first, followed by Brookins and the nuns. As Brookins stepped into the foyer, Burton got up from the chair he had been sitting in and smiled broadly.

"Not a word," Brookins commanded pointing at Burton.

"Saint Nicolas I presume?" Burton teased.

"You're lucky these kids are here or I'd break this stick over your head."

"Well the day is still young...I'd better get my helmet on just in case," Burton said as he opened the door to the courtyard. He ran around to the driver's side of the Jeep, jumped in and started the motor.

Brookins' began climbing into the Jeep but then stopped and leaned the crozier against the vehicle. He bent down, picked up the girls one at a time and placed them in the back seat of the Jeep. Then he grabbed the crozier and got into the Jeep next to Burton.

"What are you doing?" Burton asked as he feigned an indignant look at Brookins.

"What?"

"Look, if I'm gonna be driving around with Saint Nicolas, he'd better be in the back with his angels, not sitting up front with some dogface," Burton said as he motioned for Brookins to get in the back.

Brookins realized that Burton was right. He signed heavily then clambered into the back seat between the two girls, being careful not to catch the robes on anything that might tear them. Burton was about to put the Jeep into gear when Father Wolffe held up his hand.

"What's wrong Father?" Burton asked.

Father Wolffe smiled as he looked over the Jeep and its passengers.

"May God and the spirit of Saint Nicolas be with you," he said as he made the sign of the cross over the Jeep and then stepped back.

Burton nodded his thanks to the priest, and then paused to look at St. Nicolas and his angels. He smiled, put the Jeep in gear and steered out of the courtyard towards the center of town.

In the center of town, the celebration was already underway. The children and their mothers and sisters, grandparents and aunts had all gathered to await the arrival of St. Nicolas. The children, led by some of the teachers, sang songs and danced, or recited poems in honor of the good saint. One of the GIs from the 28th had a guitar and managed to strum along to their songs. Some of children even wore costumes.

Noticeably absent from the festivities were most of the fathers, uncles and older brothers. They had no doubt been taken by the Nazis and conscripted into the German army or forced to work in the labor camps. Some had been sent to concentration camps for refusing to help the Germans. Some, who were on the Gestapo's most wanted list, remained in hiding, awaiting the end of the war. Still others remained here, just outside of Wiltz, buried in the nearby cemetery.

Pvt. Burton slowed the Jeep as he approached the semicircle of people who had gathered in the square. The singing died away and the children's faces lit with excitement as the Jeep neared and everyone could finally see who was sitting in the back. Burton pulled the Jeep to a stop just in front of the group.

"Curbside service Saint Nick. Should I keep the meter running?" he quipped.

Brookins chuckled a bit, but said nothing; he was too nervous to speak. *"There's nothing to it…a pat on the head…a pinch on the cheek." That's what Harry said a few days ago when I agreed to this.* Brookins thought. It had sounded easy enough at the time, but this—this was more than he had expected. Brookins looked over the crowd and quickly estimated that there were at least sixty children…sixty pairs of eager, awestruck eyes staring back at him. And then there were the parents, beaming joyfully at St. Nicolas as their children reveled in the festivities. It was overwhelming. He reached into his pocket and pulled out a package of gum. The white gloves made it difficult to take a stick out of the pack and pull off the wrapper, but a few moments of fidgeting freed the gum and he quickly shoved it through the rope beard into his mouth. He gestured to his two angels with the package of gum, but the girls said nothing.

"Gum?" Brookins said again gesturing with the pack. Still the girls said nothing, but smiled and shook their heads.

"Sure?" Brookins asked before realizing that they probably didn't understand him.

"Uh…they're waiting for you Saint Nick," Burton interrupted.

"All right, all right," Brookins answered with a heavy sigh. As he climbed over the front seat and stepped out, he was startled to hear the children begin singing again. He started toward the group before remembering that he had left the two little girls in the Jeep. He turned back and was surprised to see that the angels had not only climbed out of the Jeep on their own but were dutifully holding the train of his robe, being careful not to let it drag on the ground. Brookins smiled nervously at the two girls and nodded in appreciation, realizing that the nuns at the convent must have instructed them. Brookins' nervousness prevented him from noticing the *Stars & Stripes* photographer who was taking pictures of the event, or the camera crew that was on hand to document the celebration.

As Brookins timidly approached the children, they sang along with the strumming guitar, but kept their eyes fixed on him, watching his every move. Brookins could read the excitement and disbelief on their faces as he, St. Nicolas, walked amongst them. Seeing St. Nicolas was something they had waited for and wished for longer than some of them could remember.

The song ended and everyone applauded. Joe Kline and Ben Kimmelman arrived carrying a tray of donuts between them. "Come and get 'em," they called, but none of the children moved. Their eyes were still fixed on St. Nicolas, as they continued to watch his every move.

"Donuts...come and get 'em," Kline repeated, his voice raised slightly in case the children hadn't heard him the first time, but still none of the children stepped forward, even at the urging of their parents. Kline and Kimmelman looked around at the crowd and then at each other, wondering why no one wanted the treats.

"Come on," Kimmelman smiled to the children as he motioned with his free arm, "Fresh donuts. They're good," he said rubbing his stomach.

"Maybe if Saint Nicolas passed out a few...?" Kline suggested.

Brookins nodded and grabbed a couple of donuts. He turned and smiled as he handed them to the child closest to him. A little boy's face glowed with excitement as he took the donuts from Saint Nicolas.

Brookins thought for a moment, trying to remember the words as he bent downcloser to the boy.

"What's your name?" he asked in German, one of a handful of phrases he had picked up while in Europe. It was all that was needed. The boy's face grew bright with delight. Saint Nicolas was speaking to *him.* The boy said something, but Brookins didn't understand him. He just smiled and patted the boy on the head, and suddenly, for the first time since he'd gotten out of the Jeep, Brookins wasn't nervous anymore.

He stood up and the semicircle quickly closed in around him. Likewise, Kline and Kimmelman were suddenly besieged with children. They handed out the donuts as fast as they could, but they were unable to keep up with the stream of eager hands. Giving up, they simply held onto the tray making sure it didn't tip over while the children helped themselves to the treats. Meanwhile, St. Nicolas walked through the crowd, meeting the children and handing out candy.

The atmosphere in the square was light and festive; the children, their parents, the nuns, and the GIs were all genuinely enjoying themselves. It had been so long since Wiltz had had the means or the opportunity to celebrate that lifting the peoples' spirits was a simple task. Wiltz had been spared the destruction brought on by the war, but it had suffered greatly from the depravity that war brings. To a people that had nothing left, the simplicity of this small Christmas party with its songs and dances, treats and candies, and the presence of St. Nicolas himself, was all that was needed to revive the joy and essence of the season. The GIs were rewarded as well. After hearing the reasons behind the St. Nicolas Day celebration, the men of the 28th Division had happily donated not only the candy from their rations, but even gifts and packages from home. Such open charity lifted their own spirits and overshadowed the disappointment of being so far from home.

For the next forty minutes or so, St. Nicolas circulated amongst the children, asking their names and passing out treats. Brookins was careful to make sure that he stopped to meet every child who was in the square, and he and the other GIs made sure each child received some sort of Christmas treat. Then it was time to head back to the castle where there would be more children waiting to meet St. Nicolas.

St. Nicolas and his angels climbed back into the Jeep and the crowd formed a procession to follow them to the castle. Burton drove as slowly as he could without stalling the Jeep, at the same time trying not to outdistance the crowd. All along the main street, children waved as the Jeep passed, eager to get St. Nicolas' attention.

Once at the castle, Burton again drove into the courtyard where the remaining children had assembled. The children were surprised not only at seeing St. Nicolas riding in the back of a Jeep, but by receiving his blessing. Brookins didn't realize he was making the sign of the cross…it hadn't been something he'd planned on doing…but after spending the past forty minutes or so with the other children, his nervousness had abated and he had fallen wholeheartedly into his role. The spirit of the moment had seized him, and before he could stop himself, his right hand was gesturing the sign of the cross over the crowd as the Jeep cleared the portal.

Burton parked the Jeep and once again St. Nicolas climbed down, his angels dutifully following behind. He confidently walked up to where an ornate red carpet had been placed on the ground. Around the edges of the carpet stood seventeen little girls, all dressed like angels, and each holding a small flag of Luxembourg. Behind the girls all the other children stood waiting. As he approached, the angels began singing a song to honor his arrival, and soon the rest of the crowd joined in. Brookins stood at the end of the carpet smiling and nodding as the children sang.

When they finished, one of the nuns from the convent stepped forward and addressed the group. Brookins didn't understand what she was saying, but as soon as she finished she approached him and motioned towards one of the Castle doors. Brookins walked slowly towards the door as the crowd began singing another song. He turned and gestured with the crozier and nodded in appreciation, knowing that they were once again singing a song to St. Nicolas.

Brookins was led into a big room just off the courtyard and seated in a large chair. He sat holding the crozier in his white-gloved hand, with his two angels standing on either side of him as the crowd made their way into the room. GIs from "the Christmas Committee" stood behind tables handing out treats, and at another table two nuns from the convent were passing out cups of hot chocolate, made from melted down chocolate bars the committee had collected.

When all the children had found a place in the great room, one of the nuns announced a series of songs, dances, and skits, all designed to honor and entertain St. Nicolas. As the children performed, Brookins and the other soldiers' hearts soared and their faces beamed with delight. This was definitely the best St. Nicolas Day celebration the children had had in years.

After the performances, the children lined up to meet and talk to St. Nicolas. One by one, they would sit on his knee and tell him what they wished for on St. Nicolas Day. Brookins didn't understand what the children were saying, but he didn't need to. In German he would ask their names and then wait for them to respond. Then he would smile and nod as if he understood every word they were saying. Occasionally he would hear the German word for mother or father, and Brookins would nod and repeat the word, helping the children to believe that he indeed knew what they were saying. After listening to their St. Nicolas Day wishes, he would kiss them on the cheek or forehead or give them a pat on the head, and they would be on their way as the next child approached. The procession had continued uninterrupted for almost an hour when Harry walked up to St. Nicolas' throne. Harry waited for St. Nicolas to finish his audience with a little boy and then quickly approached before the next child came forward.

"How's it going Saint Nick?"

"It's going pretty good. I don't know how I ever let you talk me into this Harry, but I'm glad you did."

"See…I told you it'd be fun and easy."

"I know. You were right…and these kids are great. Have you seen their faces? They're having a ball!"

"Yeah, well it seems to me that Saint Nick is too! Can I get you anything? Are you thirsty? Want some coffee or hot chocolate or something?" Stutz offered.

"No, but thanks anyway. To tell you the truth, I don't think I could keep anything down if I tried," Brookins said with his tone turning serious.

"What's the matter? You can't still be nervous…you're doing great. The kids love it."

"No it's not that, it's this hat…it's too tight! I've had the worst headache for the past two hours!" Brookins quietly explained to Stutz.

"No kidding. You'd never know it by the way you're carrying on with these kids. Have you tried stretching it out?"

"Of course…that was the first thing I did. I was able to loosen it up a bit, but I guess after wearing it for a while, sweating and all, it must have tightened up or something. It's killing me!"

"Well then take it off. No sense making yourself sick over it. Here, let me..." Stutz reached for bishop's miter.

"No don't!" Brookins exclaimed putting his hand up to stop Stutz. "Leave it alone."

"But Brooks...."

"No, leave it alone. I'll be all right."

"But if your head's pounding..."

"No, I don't want to take it off yet. If I take it off now...I don't know...it might ruin the whole Saint Nicolas thing for the kids. I can wait a while longer."

Stutz studied Brookins for a moment, without saying a word. He looked at the children waiting in line, and the people crowding the room. Everyone was smiling and laughing. Some of the children were playing games or singing, while others were enjoying their hot chocolate and candy gifts. Stutz turned back to Brookins and smiled.

"You're right, Saint Nick, I know exactly what you mean. Keep it up, you're doing great!"

"Thanks," Brookins said as Stutz turned and walked away from the throne. Brookins continued to visit with the children. Finally, after the last child had talked with St. Nicolas, the Mother Superior of the convent approached.

"Thank you for everything," she said though a heavy accent, as she took Brookins' hand in hers.

"Oh, you're welcome," Brookins replied politely.

"You and the others have been most generous. The children...they are very happy. They will remember, as will we." She looked into Brookins' eyes and squeezed his hand.

Brookins smiled at her nervously, unsure of how to react to what she had just said, or more precisely, the way she said it.

"Yes…well it was fun…it was good for us too…we're very happy," he finally stammered.

"I am sorry, but it is time. The Father…he will need the robes…for the Mass." She motioned to a door behind the chair where Brookins was sitting.

Brookins looked at the door and then back at Mother Superior; it took him a moment to understand what she meant.

"Oh of course," he said, as he got quickly to his feet and started for the door. The Mother Superior quickly caught his arm.

"One moment, please," she said and then faced the crowd. She spoke to them in Lëtzebuergesch and then, as if on cue, the children broke into another song. Brookins listened, although he didn't understand the words, and waved to everyone in the room. After about a minute, he saw the Mother Superior gesture to the door once again. Brookins turned to his two angels, who had stood by his side the entire time. He kissed each of the girls on the forehead and gave them a pat on the cheek.

"Thank you," he said to each of them in German, as he cupped their faces in his white-gloved hands. The two girls smiled back at St. Nicolas, their faces aglow with pure delight. Then Brookins turned and headed for the door. He paused in the doorway and scanned the crowd, quickly locating Harry off to one side. Harry smiled broadly, waved at St. Nicolas and gave him a "thumbs-up." Brookins smiled back and raised his right hand to his forehead in a casual salute to his friend. St. Nicolas then turned and left the room.

Brookins was surprised to find himself back in the room where he had donned the priest's robes a few hours earlier. He wasn't sure how all the rooms were connected in the castle, but somehow he was back where he had started. He let the door close behind him, then quickly removed the bishop's miter from his head. He could feel the pulse of blood rushing back into his scalp, and the indentation the hat's band had made in his skin.

"Oh *boy!* That feels better!" he sighed as the cool castle air seized his creased, sweaty brow. The nuns who were in the room to collect the robes didn't know what Brookins had said, but as they watched him rub the life back into his temples and scalp, they understood what he meant.

Brookins removed the white gloves and rope beard; the chilly air was just as refreshing on his sweaty hands and face as it had been on his head. He leaned back against the wall for a few moments, letting cool air shower over him. Then in one deft motion, he slipped the robes over his head, and handed them to one of the nuns. The other nun approached and placed a basin of warm water and a towel on the table next to Brookins. He splashed water onto his face and then buried it in the soft towel. He ran his fingers through his short hair to smooth it, straightened his uniform as best he could, and once again leaned back against the cool brick wall. As his mind wandered, taking in the day's events, he could hear the children finishing their song to St. Nicolas. Clapping and laughter followed as the party continued. Brookins rested his head against the wall; he realized the pounding headache was gone and he could feel himself smiling.

The days following the Christmas party were filled with routine tasks. The message center unit spent its time relaying messages, stringing phone lines, or doing other tedious chores that needed to be done while the division was in stand-down mode. Supplies and reinforcements continued to stream into Wiltz. The soldiers knew that when the Keystone Division was on its feet again, they would be pressed back into service, only this time they hoped the fight would take them into the heart of Germany:maybe even to Berlin and the end of the war in Europe.

For the people of Wiltz, the days following the St. Nicolas day celebrations meant a return to normalcy, or as close as they could come given the circumstances. The children returned to school, parents returned to their jobs, and thanks mostly to the soldiers of the 28th, everyone began looking forward to Christmas which was only a couple of weeks away.

Brookins spent most of his days at headquarters bent over his cryptography equipment. At night he continued to show movies to the men in his unit and other divisions located in the surrounding towns. Each time he returned from one of his trips, Brookins half-expected someone from town to stop and talk to him or thank him for being St. Nicolas, but no one ever did. After more than a week, Brookins finally realized the reason—no one from the town knew *he* was St. Nicolas. The costume, as primitive as it was, concealed his identity so thoroughly that none of the children knew it was an American soldier pretending to be St. Nicolas. When Brookins had donned the robes and later in the day taken them off, no one was around except Father Wolffe and the two nuns who had helped him. As far as the children were concerned, it *was* St. Nicolas in the castle that day.

Ten days after the party, Brookins was asked to go to Clervaux again. Another group of GIs had just been rotated out of the fighting in the Huertgen Forest and was getting some rest...along with hot showers, hot food and clean clothes. Brookins was asked to bring his film equipment and provide some entertainment for the men. The weather had been getting progressively worse over the last few days. It had turned much colder and snow was in the forecast. Brookins, as he had done many times before, sought out Keith Burton to accompany him on the trip, but Burton was no where to be found. Finally, Brookins asked Hugh Strauss to go along and drive the Jeep loaded with film equipment. Strauss was another soldier from the Signal Corps who had become a friend during basic training. Strauss was a tall, athletically built twenty-two-year-old whose passion for life was outpaced only by a gregarious demeanor to which everyone who knew him immediately surrendered. Strauss quickly agreed to go to Clervaux, knowing that it meant a couple of days of easy duty as Brookins' assistant.

On Friday morning, December 15, Brookins and Strauss loaded the equipment into the Jeep and drove off. The drive north was becoming difficult due to a light but steady rain and near freezing temperatures that turned the dirt roadways into paths of slush and mud. There was no question in either of the soldier's minds that they would be staying the night in Clervaux.

As a result of the poor road conditions, the trip took much longer than the two had expected. When they finally arrived in Clervaux, they immediately reported in at the 110th Division HQ.

"How was the ride up? I'm surprised you guys made the trip," the Captain said as he returned the salutes Brookins and Strauss offered.

"Well it wasn't easy sir, the roads are pretty bad out there," Brookins replied. "We were thinking of staying the night."

"There wouldn't be a Ritz in town by any chance?" Strauss mused.

"Sorry, the best we have to offer is the hotel at the other end of town. It's not the Ritz, but at least it's dry and warm, and I think the water is running."

"It is," replied Brookins, drawing a look of surprise from the Captain. "I was here about a week ago and stayed in that hotel." "Oh that's right. I remember now, a Bing Crosby movie wasn't it? Listen...why don't you guys go set your stuff up in the mess hall," the Captain said as he gestured with the pencil he was holding. "Remember where it is...in the hotel across the street? I assume you'll keep everything out of the way until after chow?"

"Yes sir," Brookins answered, "No problem."

"All right then, after the men finish eating you can start the show," the Captain said casually, saluting the two soldiers to end the conversation.

"Yes sir," the men answered and returned the Captain's salute.

Brookins and Strauss turned and left the HQ. As they stepped outside, they braced themselves against the cold and cutting wind.

"Let's get this stuff out of the Jeep," Brookins said as he reached in and grabbed the large, bulky wooden box containing the projector. It wasn't heavy but the protective travel case made it awkward to carry, and as it was the only 16mm projector in the sector, Brookins trusted no one with it but himself. Strauss grabbed the film canisters and the transformer and the two men walked into the hotel that had been converted into the 110th Division's mess hall. After setting the equipment in the far corner of the room, Strauss went back to the Jeep to retrieve the retractable screen, while Brookins began the task of unpacking and setting up the equipment. In no time at all, Brookins had the projector cleaned and the first reel of the film ready to load.

"Christ, it's getting cold out there," Strauss said as he returned, stomping his feet to clear the snow out of the treads in his boot. "Where should I put this?" he asked, referring to the large portable screen he was holding.

"Anywhere...we'll set that up later," Brookins replied. He turned on the transformer, and waited a few moments for it to warm up. Then he switched on the projector. It whirred and clicked noisily, as the film began to feed through the spinning sprockets, across the lens and over the sound pick-up. The audio warbled as the projector and film slowly came up to speed. Brookins switched on the projector's light and an image appeared on the wall. When the sound stabilized and the film began threading normally, he shut the machine down and quickly switched off the projector light so as to not burn the film.

"Whew...I almost forgot about that," he said to Strauss with a smile, referring to the projector lamp. "It wouldn't be good if I burned a hole through the movie."

Brookins flipped the first switch again and the film reversed. When the milk-colored leader-film appeared in the film gate, he switched off both the projector and the transformer.

"There...all set."

"That's it?" Strauss said with surprise.

"Well, after chow we'll have to set up the screen and move the projector into place, but yeah, we're all set for now. How is it outside?"

"Seems like it's getting colder. I'll bet it's reminding you of home, eh?" said Strauss.

"Yeah, a little. Wish I could be there now. I'll bet they've already got the Christmas tree up and decorated."

"Think they have some snow in Rochester by now?"

"By now?" Brookins laughed. "By now they've probably had at least two or three big storms...there's probably a couple of feet of snow on the ground. But you know, it's not the big storms that get to you. I mean, it's Rochester and it's winter. There's going to be storms. What really gets you is the lake snow. Sometimes it doesn't stop for a week and it's only maybe two or three inches a day, but then by the week's end you've got two feet of snow piled up. Then you get a storm and forget it!" Brookins expounded.

"Like I said, kind of reminds you of home," said Strauss as he motioned to the window with his head.

"Yeah, I guess it does. It sure is pretty when it first snows...but I could do without the cold."

"Yeah, speaking of the cold, how about we go to the hotel and make sure we get a room. I don't think we want to be sleeping in the Jeep tonight," Strauss said.

"Good idea," Brookins answered.

The two men walked outside, climbed into their Jeep, and headed down the street to the hotel on the other side of the small town. Inside, an old man at the front desk led them to a room on the second floor. The hotel was being used to house as much of the 110th as possible, but that was only about thirty men at any one time. Brookins and Strauss stowed their gear in the small room and hurried back down to the

Jeep. It was getting late in the day and the makeshift mess hall would soon be teaming with soldiers. Brookins and Strauss wanted to get to the hall early to get some hot food and coffee before they started the movie.

By 7:00 P.M., all the men had finished eating and it was time for the entertainment to begin. Strauss set up the folding white screen at the far end of the room while Brookins moved the film projector into place on one of the dining tables. Then, after getting a thumbs-up signal from Brookins, Strauss switched off the lights in the room and Brookins started the projector. Once again the sound warbled as the film came up to speed. The din of the mess hall quickly died away as the screen went dark and the opening credits of "Going My Way" appeared to the swell of music from the projector's small speaker. The mess hall erupted with cheers, applause and whistles as Brookins and Strauss sat back and made themselves comfortable with a couple of cups of hot coffee. Brookins would have to change film reels three times before the end of the movie; then when it was done, he'd have to restring the film, rewind it, and pack it back in the film canisters for the next showing. After that, he and Strauss would finally be able to head back to the hotel and get some sleep.

"It's a long movie and it's cold out," Strauss whispered trying not to disturb the men watching the movie. As Brookins gave him a quizzical look, Strauss reached into his inside coat pocket and pulled out a small metal flask.

"I knew there was a reason I liked having you along," Brookins said smiling widely. He held up his coffee cup. Strauss unscrewed the cap and poured from the flask, first into Brookins' cup and then into his own.

"Merry Christmas," said Strauss as the two men raised their cups in a toast.

It was just past 5:30 in the morning when Brookins and Strauss were shaken out of their sleep by what sounded like thunder. It took a moment for all of their senses to fully awaken. A much louder rumble struck, and they realized that the thunder was actually artillery shells exploding near their hotel. Another explosion shook the hotel, rattling the windows. The men saw a bright flash as the bomb hit its target. They immediately jumped out of bed and began grabbing their gear when they heard the unmistakable whistle of another shell approaching.

"Down!" Strauss yelled as the two men dove to the floor and rolled themselves as far under the beds as they could fit. The whistling sound faded for just a moment and then the shell exploded in the street in front of the hotel, blowing out the glass in the window and showering the two men with its chards.

"That was too close!" Strauss yelled through the dust and bits of ceiling debris that were pouring down on them.

"What the hell's going on?" Brookins asked out loud. He suspected he knew exactly what was happening, but he still hoped he was wrong. If the Germans were firing artillery into the town, that probably meant German infantry and armor support would soon follow.

"We've got to get out of here," Strauss announced as the two men jumped to their feet, dusted off the bits of glass, and quickly gathered their gear.

"Right…let's get to the Jeep," Brookins shouted over the sound of a more distant shell. Strauss opened the door and the two men ran down the hall to the stairway that was already clogged with GIs scrambling and yelling as they tried to get to their posts. Once outside, Brookins and Strauss jumped into their Jeep. Strauss hit the starter and despite the sub-freezing temperatures, the Jeep started on the second try.

"Atta-girl," Strauss exclaimed as he threw the Jeep into gear.

"C'mon already…let's go!" Brookins yelled over the shell bursts, the Jeep engine and the wind whistling through the Jeep's soft-cover top. "Let's get to the HQ…maybe we can find out what the hell's going on."

"Right," Strauss agreed. He drove the Jeep as fast as he could through the thick haze of smoke and mist that hovered over the snow-laden, debris-covered street. Shells continued to rain down on Clervaux as soldiers ran chaotically through the streets trying to avoid the explosions and get to their assigned positions. After about five minutes of serpentine driving, dodging soldiers, bomb craters and debris, the two men reached the 110th Division's HQ. Strauss parked the Jeep in front of the building as Brookins instinctively grabbed for his rifle in the back of the Jeep. The two hopped out and ran up the stairs and through the front doors. Once inside they quickly scanned the room for someone in command among the mass of mobilizing soldiers.

The HQ was in turmoil. Although Army Intelligence had warned front line units that the Germans may be preparing to strike in small numbers, no one had expected an attack of this magnitude. The Americans were taken by surprise and were now being forced to devise a plan on the spur of the moment to stop the German advance, at least long enough to allow the division to withdraw and regroup.

Brookins spotted the same captain the two had talked to briefly the night before.

"Captain!" Brookins called out over the roar of the room, waving his arm in an effort to get the man's attention. "Hey Captain!"

"Come on," Strauss said as he pulled on Brookins' coat. The two waded into the stream of soldiers before them.

"Hey Captain," Brookins beckoned again this time well within earshot.

Brookins and Strauss snapped the Captain a quick salute.

"Excuse me Captain…but what the hell's going on?" Strauss asked.

"What's going on?" the Captain mocked incredulously as he studied Brookins and Strauss for a moment, and then he spotted their Signal Corps patches.

"Oh, you're the movie guys...from last night, right?"

"Yes sir, Strauss and Brook...," Strauss was cut short as a shell exploded close to the HQ. "Strauss and Brookins, sir. We were at the hotel at the other end of town when the shelling started."

"Yeah, it looks like the Germans are making a push from the north. At least that's the last report we had. The shelling has cut the lines so we've lost telephone communications with the forward OPs. All we have now are field radios, and there just aren't enough of them out there right now. It looks as though the Krauts are trying to make a push through our lines...but we're not sure what units they've got."

The Captain stopped short as the whistle of another shell grew louder then suddenly went silent. The men in the room unconsciously hunched over and held onto their helmets. The building shook violently as the shell exploded somewhere in the street, not far away. Several men were knocked off their feet by the concussion and part of the ceiling came crashing down at the rear of the room, but luckily no one was hurt.

"Sons of bitches," the Captain yelled angrily. "Anyway, we think it might be elements of the 7th Army and 5th Panzer Division. At least that's the bit of intelligence we received before the lines went dead," he explained. "Wait, did you say you guys just came from the hotel?"

"Yes sir, on the other end of town," Strauss replied.

"Was there anybody else in there? Did everyone get out?

"I'm not sure Captain. We got outside, hopped in the Jeep and came right here. It looked like everyone was on the move though," Brookins explained.

"Look, I need you guys to get back to that hotel and make sure everyone's out...you got it!" the Captain ordered.

"Yes sir," Strauss and Brookins chorused with obvious apprehension.

"Look, I know you two want to get back to your unit," the Captain pressed, "but I need you to go back there first and give the word for everyone to get out of the building. Tell whoever's there to rally here at HQ, got it?"

"Got it," Strauss answered.

"Frankly we don't know what's going on and I don't want anyone left behind."

"So we're pulling out then?" Brookins asked.

"Look, we're spread kind of thin, you know? Just get to that hotel and make sure everyone's out, understand?" The Captain saluted, putting an end to any further discussion.

"Yes sir," the two replied and returned the salute.

They turned and quickly made their way to the door, braced themselves against the cold as they stepped outside and began trotting down the stairs. Suddenly both men stopped in their tracks.

"The Jeep! Where the hell is the Jeep?" Strauss yelled.

The Jeep had vanished from the front of the hotel where they had parked. The two men scanned up and down the street but there was no sign of it.

"Christ!" Brookins exclaimed. "It had all my equipment in it!"

"Your equipment?" yelled Strauss through the chaos that engulfed the town. "To hell with your equipment. My rifle was in that Jeep! And how the hell are we supposed to get back to Wiltz now?"

Brookins and Strauss heard another whistle and without a word they, and everyone around them, dove into the snow for cover. The shell hit the top of the building across from the HQ. When the subsequent shower of debris had ended, the soldiers jumped to their feet, and for a moment no one moved. Each man realized how close the shell had hit. Amazingly, no one had been injured by the explosion or the falling rubble. Then, as if on cue, the running, yelling, and mayhem continued.

Brookins and Strauss jogged down the street towards the hotel. As daylight began to grow, the two men pushed through the deep snow and thickening haze, and the maze of men and machinery now choking the streets. It took nearly ten minutes for the two men to reach the hotel. They entered the foyer, which was unexpectedly void of activity, and paused for a few moments to catch their breath.

"Hey!" Brookins finally shouted into the small lobby. "Is anyone in here?"

"Hello? Anyone here?" Strauss yelled. They waited for an answer, but none came.

"There's no one here! Let's get back to the command post," Brookins scowled in exasperation. The two men turned and ran back out of the hotel and into the street. Strauss stopped short and put out his hand to stop Brookins who was running a few feet behind.

"Christ...look!" Strauss said, pointing to a hillside just beyond the edge of town. Through breaks in the now rolling smoke and mist, Strauss and Brookins could see scores of men, their gray uniforms standing out against the snow covered hills, rapidly moving towards Clervaux. They couldn't see the Panzer support tanks the Captain had mentioned, but both men knew the massive machines were probably right behind the advancing infantry.

"They're coming on fast," Brookins said anxiously.

"Forget command..." Strauss declared, "we need to get out of here now!"

"But where to?"

"Let's head south. We've got to try to get back to Wiltz," Strauss said.

"In this weather and without the Jeep? Are you nuts? It'll take forever...and that's if we don't run into any Germans."

"Do you have a better idea?" replied Strauss, gesturing to the now fog-eclipsed hillside.

Brookins glanced at the hillside where he knew the German troops were advancing.

"Wiltz it is," he said and the two of them headed out of town.

Their progress was slowed by the deep snow and thick fog. They took frequent breaks, although they never rested too long, knowing that the Germans might be right behind them, or for that matter, in front of them. The fact was, they had no idea exactly where the Germans were. The only thing they knew for sure was that they were heading back to Wiltz. As they traveled further and further from town, the sound of gunfire and artillery began to fade. They began to reason that the German attack was probably focused on Clervaux, and that they'd be safe as long as they kept heading south. They had no idea of the enormity of the German assault.

They had gone about five miles when they heard a dull rumbling sound ahead of them. As the sound grew louder they realized it was an engine working hard to make its way along the slippery, hilly road. They hoped it was an American truck or Jeep, or even a Sherman tank on its way to reinforce the troops at Clervaux, but there was no way to know until they actually saw it. To be safe, the men needed cover until they could identify the fast approaching vehicle. About fifty yards ahead and just off the road was a farmhouse. Smoke coming from the chimney suggested that it was occupied, but it was the only place the men would be able to get to in time to hide.

"Quick...in there," Brookins said as he pushed Strauss, urging him forward. The two of them ran for the house. As they closed the distance, they slowed down to approach more cautiously. They glanced at each other, silently synchronized their movements, and crept towards the door, peering in through the front windows to see if anyone was inside. Seeing no one, they paused on either side of the door. Strauss nodded to Brookins who clicked off the safety of his M-1 rifle—the only weapon they had—and raised it to his shoulder, keeping the muzzle pointed down. Strauss then took a deep breath, and in one fluid motion, stepped to the door and kicked it as hard as he could, hitting it squarely beside the knob. The door swung open as Strauss retreated to the side for cover. Brookins raised the barrel of the gun, dropped to one knee and swung his body around the doorway, panning the rifle across the room as he looked for any sign of movement. Seeing none, he stood up and moved cautiously into the room, still sweeping the M-1 from side to side. Except for a large well-worn table and a wooden chair, the room was empty; the house had apparently not been lived in for quite some time. Brookins turned back to Strauss who was keeping an eye on the road.

"Come on…it's clear," he said.

Strauss ducked inside and closed the door. The pair stood off to the side of the windows, watching to see whatever was coming up the road. As they waited, the sound of creaking treads began to blend with the dull hum of the engine. Finally, through the fog they spotted a black cross painted on the hood of a German halftrack, behind which followed at least thirty German soldiers.

"Damn it," Strauss whispered as he and Brookins ducked below the window and leaned close to the wall. Strauss nodded towards a door at the back of the room. "Let's get out of here!"

The two men, still crouching, retreated towards the back of the small house. They could hide in the back they thought in case the Germans took an interest in the house and stopped to check. All the Germans would see would be an empty room, and perhaps they'd pass by the house, but when Brookins opened the door to the back room, the thick, black smoke the men had seen from the road, began to roll in. The house had been hit by a mortar shell and the back half of it was on fire.

"Damn!" Brookins said quickly closing the door. "Get back!"

The two men scurried to the front of the burning house and crouched below the windows at the back side of the door. If the Germans stopped to check the house now, Brookins and Strauss would have no place to hide and nowhere to run. As the sound of the German halftrack rumbled by, Brookins slid his hand from the side of the M-1 to the trigger. In his mind, he imagined the Germans opening the door and entering the house to find him and Strauss huddled in the corner. As the scene played out in his mind he knew that after a volley of shots, the Germans would overwhelm them, and they would surely be killed.

He moved his finger from the trigger, and flipped on the safety. Hearing the familiar click, Strauss looked at him for a moment and then nodded. Brookins now began to imagine the Germans passing the house and seeing that it was on fire. They might think the house was badly damaged and that anyone living there was certainly gone by now. Plus, he thought, the Germans were on the move and stopping to check out a small, burning farmhouse would only slow them down. These were all logical assumptions he thought; he just hoped the Germans were being logical.

The sound of the rumbling halftrack, mixed with the voices of the German soldiers, alerted Brookins and Strauss that the enemy was passing directly in front of them. As Strauss huddled close to the wall, he heard the sound of footsteps approaching the farmhouse and gently snapped his fingers to signal Brookins. The two men crouched as low as they could, trying to remove themselves from the view of the windows. Just outside the farmhouse door, a German soldier began yelling. The soldier's call was answered by a distant voice, and almost immediately, Strauss and Brookins heard the footsteps retreat. A few more moments passed while the huddled men remained completely still, holding their breath and straining to hear. The fading engine seemed to imply that the Germans had bypassed the burning farmhouse and were continuing up the road, just as Brookins had imagined. Still, there was no way to be sure until they looked, and they had no intention of doing so until the sound of the rumbling engine had faded completely. Five minutes passed like an eternity for the frightened men. Finally, when they could no longer hear the vehicle, Strauss slowly rose up to look out the window. With his eyes barely above the edge of the sill, he looked to the left, up the road from where he and Brookins had come, and saw the last of the gray uniforms disappear into the thin rolling mist. Then he looked to the right and saw only the road.

"Well?" Brookins whispered.

Strauss continued scanning the area in front of the farmhouse, straining to see through the curtain of mist.

"I think it's clear. I don't see anything...just snow and pine trees."

The two men slowly got to their feet. Strauss cautiously opened the door, and peered out, making sure the road was indeed clear. When he was satisfied, he stepped outside, paused for a moment, and then waved for Brookins to come out. They stood just outside the burning farmhouse, studying the surrounding countryside.

"They passed us by," an amazed Brookins said as he began to grin. "The sons-of- bitches passed us right by!"

The pair stood in the doorway of the farmhouse unaware of the cold or the biting wind or even the spray of freezing mist each gust of wind delivered. They stood warm and relieved as they contemplated just how close they had come to being captured if not killed by the enemy.

"Today must be our lucky day," Strauss said humbly.

The two men quickly mapped out their surroundings and got their bearings, and then bundled themselves against the cold breeze, and started back down the road to Wiltz. They'd gone only a few hundred yards when they crested a hill and stumbled upon two German soldiers setting up an MG-42 machine gun. The Germans, partially cloaked by the mist, were no more than twenty yards away and were as startled to see the American soldiers, as Brookins and Strauss were to see them. The four men stood overcome by surprise and frozen with fear, staring at each other as seconds crept by. In another time and another place, they might have raised a glass together as friends instead of raising weapons as enemies, but in this awkward moment frozen in time, the men now faced each other as duty-bound soldiers on opposite sides of a war.

The Germans, who hadn't finished setting up their machine gun yet, quickly reached for their rifles.

Brookins moved equally as fast and without thought, raised the M-1 to his shoulder as the unarmed Strauss dove to the ground for cover. Brookins began pulling the trigger as fast as he could and yelling to scare away the fear of shooting and of being shot. When the spent ammunition clip ejected from the rifle he stopped, but the sound of the shots hung in the thick air and seemed to echo endlessly through the woods and surrounding hills. As the smoke cleared beyond the front sight on Brookins' rifle, he could see the two Germans slumped over their machine gun.

"Nice going Brooks," Strauss praised as he sprung to his feet and wiped the snow off his uniform.

Brookins stood stunned and numb, breathing heavily. His heart raced as he looked at the heaped bodies of the German soldiers.

"Are you hit?" Strauss asked.

Brookins said nothing, his blank stare fixed on the German soldiers.

"Brooks! Are you hit?"

"What?" Brookins replied, blinking away the water in his eyes. "No, I'm not..."

"Then come on, let's go!" Strauss said as he started off down the road.

He'd gone a few steps before he realized that Brookins hadn't moved.

"Brooks! Let's go!" Strauss called to his friend imploringly. He quickly walked back and tugged at Brookins' arm.

"Come on, we have to get going. Someone had to hear the shooting. What if that halftrack comes back or there're other Krauts around?"

Brookins slowly pulled his gaze away from the soldiers he had just shot and looked at Strauss. Strauss could read the confusion and regret in Brookins' face, but could only imagine the emotions that were raging within him.

"Look Brooks..." Strauss began, trying to comfort his friend. He glanced over at the German soldiers and then back at Brookins. "Look...you had to do it. They would have killed us for sure, you know that."

"Sure, but I never..."

"Forget it, Brooks," Strauss interrupted. "It had to be done, we're in a war. That's all there is to it."

"Do you think they're dead?"

"I don't know; I guess so," Strauss said anxiously.

"You ever shot anyone before...ever killed anyone?" Brookins asked in a distant voice.

"No Brooks...never, but if I was in your shoes...I'd have done just what you did. Now let's get out of here before this place is crawling with Krauts."

Brookins seemed to finally get control of himself. He knew Strauss was right. The Germans would have certainly shot the two of them. After all, they were setting up a machine gun; there was no telling how many other GIs would have run into that gun, Brookins reasoned. He reached into the pocket of his coat and pulled out another clip of bullets. He braced the butt of his rifle against the thigh of his leg, pushed the clip into the breach and slammed the bolt shut. Then he took a deep breath and exhaled. "Ok, let's go."

He headed off after Strauss, but he turned one last time, and trotting backwards down the road, gave the Germans one last look. Through the thickening mist he saw one of the soldiers roll over onto his side and raise his hand slightly. Brookins turned back to the road and hung his head, but he kept moving. In his heart he was hoping and praying that the two soldiers were still alive.

By noon, the fog and mist began to thin, but there were still gray skies and cold temperatures. Both Brookins and Strauss were exhausted from moving through the deep snow along the twenty-mile trek back to Wiltz. They had paused for a few minutes to rest, when they again heard the sound of an engine. The two men stood on the tree lined roadside, straining to hear as the engine's dull rumbling reverberated through the rolling countryside. The sound seemed to be coming from all around them. Finally as it grew stronger, they could tell that it was approaching from the road behind them.

"Quick...cover," Strauss said nudging Brookins into the woods.

The two men crouched down behind some snow-covered brush, and waited for the vehicle to come into view. It seemed as though neither man breathed. Finally through the brush, they spotted two olive green trucks with red crosses painted on the hoods and sides.

"They're ours!" Brookins exclaimed. The two men jumped up from their hiding place and ran through the snow to the roadside, yelling and waving their arms at the approaching ambulances.

The ambulances came to a stop just beyond the two men.

"Hey...are we ever glad to see you," Strauss greeted as he trotted up to the driver of the lead vehicle. "We've been hiking down this road for hours."

"You guys look frozen," the driver said. "Where'd you come from?"

"Clervaux," Strauss answered.

"Clervaux?" the driver responded with surprise, as he glanced over at the soldier in the cab next to him, "Clervaux's a mess!"

"What do you mean 'a mess'," asked Strauss.

"The last we heard, the Krauts were hitting pretty hard up there. Someone said they had the place just about surrounded," the driver explained. "The word is they're pushing through our lines all over the place and up in Clervaux it's pretty bad."

Brookins and Strauss looked at each other, both thinking how lucky they were to have made it out of the town at all.

"Where are you guys heading," the driver asked.

"Wiltz," answered Brookins. "Think we can get a lift?"

"Sure, but not with that," replied the driver, gesturing to Brookins' rifle.

"What do you mean...why not," asked the puzzled Brookins.

"Red Cross regulations. No weapons. It's an ambulance," the man said pointing at the faded insignia on the truck's hood.

Brookins and Strauss were dumbfounded. Certainly they wanted and needed to get back to Wiltz and their division's HQ, especially since they'd been walking for hours through heavy snow and freezing temperatures. They were tired, cold, hungry, and still a long way from Wiltz. There was no telling when or if they would encounter another Allied vehicle, let alone one that was heading into town. And then there were the Germans to think about. What would they do if they ran into more Germans without the only weapon they had between them? No doubt they would be forced to surrender, or worse.

"Hey guys, let's go," the driver interrupted their thoughts. "It's not getting any warmer out here and there're guys in the back. Do you want a ride into Wiltz or not."

"Sure we want a ride but I don't think we should leave behind the only weapon we have," Brookins answered. "We've already run into some Krauts on this road."

"Look pal, it's the rules," the driver stressed.

"Rules?" Strauss lashed out. "Who cares about rules! You just got through saying that the Krauts are on the move and they're pouring through our lines. Do you think they're worried about the rules?"

"Look, pal, if it was up to me I'd say no problem. But it ain't up to me. I've got to follow orders you know. No weapon or no ride, that's it," the driver stated emphatically.

Strauss and Brookins looked at each other, each waiting for the other to decide what to do.

"Fine, have it your way, but we're not giving up the only rifle we have," Strauss finally blurted out

"All right, suit yourself," the driver said as he shifted the ambulance into gear and started down the road, with the second ambulance right behind.

"Do you believe those guys," Strauss commented as they watched the ambulances drive out of sight.

"You think we did the right thing?" asked Brookins.

"After what happened this morning? You're dammed right we did the right thing. We'll get to Wiltz eventually...somehow. Those guys can't be the only GIs on this road."

"Let's hope not. We should have asked them how far it was to Wiltz," Brookins realized.

"Ah damn...you're right."

"Well...no sense waiting around here. I don't think the next bus is due for awhile," Brookins tried to joke.

Once again Brookins and Strauss started walking. They had been alone on the road for an hour when suddenly they were startled by the sound of another engine. This time the vehicle approached too quickly for them to seek cover. By the time they heard the moan of the engine, it was coming up the road behind them. The vehicle rounded a bend and suddenly, fear melted to relief as they saw an American army truck barreling down the muddied road. The driver had already seen them and was downshifting.

"Where are you guys heading?" inquired the driver as he brought the truck to a stop.

"Wiltz!" Strauss announced. "Are you heading that way?"

"We sure are...you guys need a lift?"

"Do we ever!"

"Well hop in...we'll have you there in no time," the driver said.

"Have you seen any Germans?" Strauss asked.

"Germans?" The driver seemed surprised by the question.

"Yeah...Germans," Strauss repeated. "They're on the move."

"Who's on the move?" the man asked dumbfounded.

It was suddenly more than Strauss could take and he lashed out sarcastically at the man.

"The Krauts! You've heard of them, right? They're the reason we're over here!"

"Are you sure? We haven't heard anything about it."

"Look," Brookins broke in. "We need to get to Wiltz, can we get a ride into town with you guys?"

"Yeah, Sure," the driver said realizing that Strauss and Brookins were serious about the German attack. "Go ahead, hop in, there's still plenty of room."

"Thanks!" Brookins said as he and Strauss hustled to the back of the truck. Brookins lifted up the canvas flap that covered the back of the truck.

"What the hell is this?" Strauss asked as he looked into the truck bed. He was still a bit frazzled. "I don't believe it...it's a dammed laundry truck."

"Well, let's look at the bright side. At least it's clean laundry," said Brookins.

They climbed in past the flap and Brookins hit the deck of the truck bed twice with the butt of his gun to signal the driver.

"Well, it's cold and it *was* a long walk," Strauss said reaching into his coat pocket and pulling out his metal flask as the truck jerked forward. He unscrewed the cap and tried to see what was left in the flask, but it was too dark inside the truck. Instead he swished around the contents, and satisfied with his findings, raised the flask to his lips. Then he handed the flask over to Brookins who raised it in a toast.

"Merry Christmas," Brookins said and tilted his head back. He could feel the warmth of the alcohol slide down his throat and into his stomach.

"Someday you'll have to tell me what's in that," he said as he handed the flask back to Strauss.

Strauss took another drink and put the cap back on the flask. "Someday," he smiled, as he collapsed onto the pile of soft, clean clothes.

The 28th Infantry Division marches down the Champs Elysees; August 29, 1944

Courtesy of the US Army/National Archives

Celebrating the liberation of Wiltz; September 10, 1944

Courtesy of the Battle of the Bulge Museum, Wiltz

American soldiers fighting in the Huertgen Forest November 1944

Courtesy of the US Army/National Archives

General Eisenhower visits the soldiers in Wiltz; November 12, 1944

Courtesy of the Battle of the Bulge Museum, Wiltz

Richard Brookins, The American St. Nicolas, rides to the center of Wiltz accompanied by his two angels; December 5th, 1944

Courtesy of the US Army/National Archives

The American St. Nicolas greets a little boy in Wiltz; December 5, 1944

Courtesy of the Oeuvre St. Nicolas, Wiltz

The American St. Nicolas Walking with Father Wolffe; December 5, 1945

Courtesy of the Oeuvre St. Nicolas, Wiltz

The American St. Nicolas accompanied by Father Wolffe, at the Wiltz Castle meeting another group of children; December 5, 1945

Courtesy of the US Army/National Archives

The children singing a song welcoming St. Nicolas in the Wiltz Castle courtyard; December 5, 1945
Courtesy of the US Army/National Archives

The American St. Nicolas in the Wiltz castle; December 5, 1944
Courtesy of the Oeuvre St. Nicolas, Wiltz

This Bazooka team emerges from the woods outside of Wiltz after being on guard over night at the beginning of the Battle Of The Bulge; December 1944

Courtesy of the US Army/National Archives

This photo is of a German soldier carrying ammunition during the Battle Of The Bulge. It came from captured German film; December 1944

Courtesy of the US Army/ National Archives

German prisoners being marched out of town following the fall of Aachen; December 1944

Courtesy of the US Army/ National Archives

German soldiers captured in the Ardennes during the Battle Of The Bulge; January 1945

Courtesy of the US Army/National Archives

Rue Des Tondeurs, Wiltz
January 1945
Courtesy of the Battle of the Bulge Museum, Wiltz

Town Hall of Wiltz
January 1945
Courtesy of the Battle of the Bulge Museum, Wiltz

The Boys School in Wiltz after the Battle of the Bulge, January 1945. On this site now stands the National monument to the general strike
Courtesy of the Battle of the Bulge Museum, Wiltz

Richard Brookins in Germany; May 1945
Courtesy of the Private Collection of Richard Brookins

Richard Brookins in Germany; May 1945
Courtesy of the Private Collection of Richard Brookins

JULY, 1977

It was almost eleven o'clock at night when a taxi dropped Frank McClelland off in front of his house. Frank had left Germany earlier that day and spent the better part of twelve hours in either an airplane or an airport, but now, finally, he was home.

Frank paid the driver, then picked up his one suitcase and marched up to the front door. He propped the storm door open with his foot as he pushed a key into the deadbolt, only to find that the lock wouldn't budge. Mumbling in frustration, he dropped his suitcase on the front stoop and gave the doorknob a sharp pull as he twisted the key. It now moved freely, reeling in the deadbolt. He opened the heavy door to the sound of crunching just inside the foyer. Frank rolled his eyes as his remembered that he hadn't made it to the post office to put his mail on hold before leaving. He picked up his suitcase and stepped in across the pile of mail as he felt along the wall for the light switch. He flipped on the light in the foyer. The house had an empty stale smell from being closed up for ten days. Frank dropped his suitcase on top of the mail pile and walked across the living room. Having no air conditioner, he opened a couple of windows on the side of the house, letting the air of the summer night cool and revive the stale rooms. Back in the foyer, he picked up his suitcase and climbed the stairs to the bedroom. The mail would still be there in the morning he thought, for now all he wanted to do was to get a solid night's sleep in his own bed.

Inside the bedroom, Frank opened his suitcase and hastily unpacked, throwing nearly all the clothing into the hamper except for a few clean pairs of socks and underwear. He carried his shaving kit into the bathroom and put the contents in their usual places.

Returning to the bedroom, Frank set the suitcase aside and opened one of the windows. He closed his eyes and breathed in the fresh night air scented with honeysuckle that grew wild along the fence in his yard. He flopped onto the bed. Despite the house being closed up, the fresh sheets he'd put on the day he left for Europe, seemed cool and comforting. Tomorrow he would go through the mail on the foyer floor, but for now he just wanted to sleep. He sighed, closed his eyes, and in a few minutes was fast asleep.

The next morning Frank woke up and realized he had fallen asleep in his clothes. He hadn't planned on doing that, but the traveling and jet lag had gotten the better of him. He went downstairs to the kitchen and started a pot of coffee before jumping into the shower and putting on some clean clothes. After dressing, he returned to the kitchen, this time stopping at the foyer to pick up the mail piled on the floor. As he sat at the kitchen table with his coffee he sorted through the mail, separating out the bills and other important letters. Everything else went into the nearby trash can unopened. Tomorrow was Tuesday and he'd be going back to his job as a safety inspector for the Pittsburgh Railroad; but for today, the last day of his vacation, there was laundry and shopping to do, as well as paying some of the bills he'd just opened. He also wanted to get his suitcase back into the attic before the summer sun began beating down on the slate roof and the attic became too hot. The last place Frank wanted to be on a hot summer day was in the attic. He went upstairs and grabbed the suitcase from under the window where he'd left it. Carrying the bag to the closet, he pulled a dangling string to turn on the light and pushed aside the clothes at one end of the closet. Behind the clothing lay a small landing and above it, framed into the ceiling, was a piece of painted plywood. Frank positioned himself on the landing to get some leverage and pushed at the center of the plywood moving the board upward until it cleared the attic floorboards. He then slid the piece of plywood to the right along the attic floor. It was mid-morning and already Frank could feel hot, stifling air collecting in the recess above him. He reached up and pulled at the string to turn on the attic light. He then hopped down from the landing and grabbed the suitcase. Hoisting the bag up on to the landing, he opened it one more time to make sure he'd taken everything out before storing it. He felt around in the inner pockets to make sure they were empty too. As he did, he came across a folded piece of notepaper. He unfolded the paper and suddenly remembered that it had been given to him by one of the men he'd met in Wiltz. He opened it and read the name "Karl Mueller" along with an address and a telephone number. Frank stuffed the paper into his shirt pocket and closed the suitcase before shoveing it through the opening in the ceiling. It landed with a thud on the attic floor. Frank switched off the lights and closed everything up again before heading back down to the kitchen table. There at the table, he pulled the crumpled paper from his pocket and smoothed it out. On the bottom half of the paper under Mueller's name and address were the words, "Richard Brookins, Rochester."

Frank sat back in his chair contemplating what to do. He had promised the men in Luxembourg that he would try to find Brookins when he returned home, but now he wasn't sure how to go about it; all he had was a thirty-year-old name and a town. As he pondered, his gaze fell on the telephone bill he'd just opened. Frank's mind raced as he reached into a cupboard drawer just under the phone and retrieved an old address book stuffed thick with so many scraps of paper that it barely closed. He opened the book and began sorting through the yellowed pieces of paper until he found the one he wanted. Then he grabbed for the phone on the kitchen wall and began dialing. The phone rang several times before there was a click and a voice on the other end.

"Bell of Pennsylvania...how may I direct your call?"

"Extension 219, please," Frank said. There was a series of clicks on the line.

"John Vrabel," another voice declared.

"Johnny...it's Frank McClelland. How have you been?" Frank asked his old schoolmate.

"Frankie!...how the hell are ya?" Johnny said with surprise.

"Fine, fine. How are you doing?"

"Great, thanks. I haven't heard from you in...Christ, how long has it been?"

"Yeah, I know. It's been awhile. I think the last time was at Butya's Bar, remember?"

"Butya's? No I don't. Wait! I remember now. That's right. Some big shot's retirement party or something, right?"

"That's right. We had a party for one of the guys I worked with at the railroad. We ran into each other there. How have you been?"

"Things are good...can't complain. How about you? Hey, I was awfully sorry to hear about Martha."

"Thanks. Yeah it was bad...the cancer just ate her up. But, God rest her soul, she's not suffering anymore," said Frank, mournfully thinking of his wife.

"She was a fine woman, Frank. Like I said, I was awfully sorry when I heard about it."

"Well thanks, Johnny, I appreciate that," Frank said solemnly and then cleared his throat. "Listen, the reason I'm calling...you obviously still work for the phone company, right?"

"Sure...almost twenty years now, why? You looking for a job?" Vrabel kidded.

"Sure, I'd like something that pays a hundred grand a year, but I only want to work three days a week...and only from eleven to one," Frank laughed. "Actually the real story is...well it's kind of hard to explain, but I was wondering if you could help me find a guy."

"Find a guy? You mean a number? Have you tried information?"

"Well no I haven't," Frank began to explain. "You see I just came back from Europe..."

"No kidding!" Vrabel interjected with genuine surprise.

"Yeah, I just got back yesterday. I visited a bunch of places...kind of retracing my steps from during the war. I always said I was going to do it someday, and with Martha gone and the kids on they're own, well I figured what the hell."

"No kidding...how was it?"

"It was good. I went to Germany, France, Belgium and Luxembourg. I rented a car and just drove all over."

"Gee Frankie...that sounds great."

"Oh it was...but here's the thing...while I was in Luxembourg, I ran into these locals over there and...well to make a long story short...I told them I'd help find this guy that served over there during the war. The problem is, all I've got is a name and the town where he lived thirty years ago."

"Wait…I don't get it. You need to find someone from a town over in Europe?" a confused Vrabel asked.

"No, no…the guy they're looking for is American…he was a GI over there during the war. We were in the same outfit, though I didn't know him. Anyway, some of the people of this one town asked me if I would help them try to find this guy. They figured that since we were in the same unit maybe I'd have better luck tracking him down," Frank explained.

"Are you kidding?"

"No! They really want to find this guy. Like I said, it's sort of a long story. And honestly I don't even know if this guy made it out of the war…and even if he did, I don't know if he's in the same town. So I didn't think I could just call information, you know? Then I remembered that you worked for the phone company and I thought maybe you'd be able to feed the name into a computer or something."

"I'd like to help you out Frank, but they don't let us use phone company records for personal use. They've got some serious rules against that sort of thing," Vrabel explained.

"Oh, I didn't realize. Well look…I don't want to get you in any trouble or anything. Like I said, I was just trying to help out these guys in Luxembourg. They're the ones who really wanted to find this guy, because of what he did for them during the war I guess."

"So what's the story with this guy? Is he Audie Murphy or something? What'd he do…win the war?"

"Well, like I said it's a long story but..."

"Listen Frankie, I tell you what...I can't do anything right now. I'm in the middle of something, but why don't you give me the guy's name and address or whatever you have, and I'll see what I can do. I can't promise you anything. Like I said, I really shouldn't be doing this sort of thing."

"Thanks Johnny, whatever you can do would be great," Frank said. "The guy's name is Richard Brookins and he came from Rochester, New York."

"You'd better give me your number again, too. I know I have it at home but not here at the office. Now, this may take some time, but I'll let you know what I find out either way, ok?"

"Sounds great, Johnny," Frank said and then recited his phone number. "Thanks a bunch. Beers at Butya's on me next time, ok?"

"I'm going to hold you to that!" Vrabel joked.

"You got it. Thanks again John," Frank said as he hung up the phone.

As far as Frank was concerned, he had now done what he had promised. He told Karl Mueller that he would try to find Brookins once he returned home, and now he had.

Frank put the yellowed scrap of paper that held John Vrabel's name and phone number back in the address book and returned the book to the drawer. There were plenty of chores he needed to do before returning to work the following day. On a piece of scrap paper he began jotting down a list of things he would need from the grocery store. He took a moment to clear the refrigerator of everything he thought had spoiled while he was away and checked the results against his list. Then he went upstairs to grab the clothes hamper out of the bedroom. As Frank descended the stairs, he tried to organize the day in his mind, starting with the laundry. After loading a pile of clothes into the washing machine, he would go to the grocery store and get what he needed. By that time the clothes would be done and he could throw them into the dryer. Then he planned to go outside and mow the overgrown lawn.

Frank hauled the hamper down to the basement and dumped its contents onto the cellar floor. He opened the shut-off valves mounted on the basement wall and pulled the knob on the washing machine to turn on the water. As the tub began filling he added the detergent and clothes. He always used warm water in the wash cycle and cold in the rinse cycle, that way he thought, he wouldn't have to sort out the whites and the colors. He could just throw everything in together and wash it all at once. Frank closed the lid of the washing machine just as the phone on the kitchen wall began ringing. He sprinted up the stairs to the kitchen and grabbed at the handset.

"Hello?" he barked into the phone with an obviously winded voice.

"Frank? Is that you?" the voice on the other end of the line asked.

"Yes, who's this?"

"It's John! Don't tell me you forget already!" John Vrabel prodded.

"No…no. Sorry John, I just ran up from the basement. I didn't recognize your voice," Frank explained.

"Listen I did a quick check on that name you gave me, and you're not going to believe this…your boy is alive and well, and get this, he's still in Rochester."

"Are you kidding me?"

"Well, let me clarify," Vrabel began. "There is a Richard Brookins who lives in Rochester. Now, I don't know if this is the guy you're looking for or not, but that's what the computer spit out. "

"Holy cow, I can't believe you found the number so fast," Frank said.

"Well to be honest with you, it wasn't too hard. Get this, your guy actually works for the phone company!"

"No kidding?"

"Yeah…and it's probably a good thing you called me since his number's unlisted. Even if you called information, they wouldn't have been any help to you."

"How do we know this is the right guy?" Frank quizzed.

"Well, we don't. I mean it could be a relative, maybe a son or something, you never know. Remember…all you gave me was a name and city and that's what I ran through the computer. What came back doesn't say how old the person is or anything like that…and I'm not about to go searching through company records…at least not any more than I already have."

"Hey…at least it's a place to start." Frank said.

John read the man's phone number and address to Frank, who copied it down and just to be sure, read it back to John.

"Ok…remember, you owe me beers at Butya's."

"Sure Johnny, you can count on it," Frank assured him cheerfully. "I'll buy you the whole keg. Thanks for the help...I really appreciate it."

"No problem. Maybe when we're having those beers you can fill me in on what this is all about."

"You've got a deal. Thanks again...we'll see ya."

Frank sat down at the kitchen table and stared at the number he had just written down. He wondered what to do next. He hadn't thought that far ahead since he really hadn't believed he'd be able to find Richard Brookins, let alone get a phone number and an address. Frank thought about writing a letter to Brookins, explaining his trip and the promise he had made, but he wasn't much of a letter writer; perhaps a phone call would be better. Frank rehearsed his part of the conversation several times, trying to get the words just right. After about twenty minutes he looked at the clock on the kitchen wall. He thought for a moment and then finally picked up the phone and dialed.

"Operator," a voice announced.

"Yes...I'd like to make a long distance call...to Luxembourg."

The phone rang at about a quarter past eight in the morning. After the fourth ring, Dick Brookins, who had been standing in front of a mirror tying his tie, grabbed the handset off the phone by the bed.

"Hello?" he called into handset, slightly annoyed by the early morning call.

There was silence on the line, punctuated by static, and Brookins thought that perhaps the person on the other end had not heard him.

"Hello?" he repeated his voice a bit louder.

"Yes," an accent-laden voice answered. "Mister Richard Brookins please."

"Yes that's me, who is this?"

"Oh...Mister Brookins, yes?"

"Yes, that's correct," Brookins responded in a louder and clearer tone.

"Ah Mister Brookins, my name is Karl Mueller and I am calling to you from Wiltz in Luxembourg."

Brookins stood silent as a sudden surge of emotion overwhelmed him. Like a movie playing in his head, a random web of wartime memories ran through his mind. Some he chose to recall; others he had tried to forget. There was Wiltz and Luxembourg, and Paris and Normandy. There was Harry Stutz and Hugh Strauss, the Huertgen Forest and the Bulge, and the Germans. There was the cold, the heat, the smells and the sounds, the movies and the message center, and always the bombs and the shooting. Decades had passed since he'd thought about any of those things, except of course for the yearly Veteran's Day parade in which he always participated.

"Hello? Are you still there?" Mueller asked, quickly halting the barrage of splintered memories that assaulted Brookins.

"Uh...yes, I am. I'm sorry...did you say you were calling from Wiltz in Luxembourg?"

"Yes that is correct. You are Richard Brookins, yes?"

"Yes that's right," Brookins replied.

"And were you with the American army during the war?" Mueller questioned in a tone that implied more queries were coming.

"Yes I was," Brookins answered with reservation. "What's this all about?" he asked anxiously.

"Ah yes...please, one more question. Were you in Wiltz during the war?"

"Yes I was," Brookins said impatiently. "Look…what's all this…"

"Well then," Mueller interrupted, "you are the soldier who was Saint Nicolas…in Wiltz…for the children. You are the American Saint Nicolas," Mueller announced jubilantly

Brookins was speechless. He sat down on the bed as a picture flashed across his mind; a picture that his mother had clipped from the *Rochester Democrat* newspaper showing him dressed as St. Nicolas and riding in an army Jeep through the town of Wiltz; the same picture that was in an edition of the *Stars & Stripes* that had been stored away in a decades-old footlocker up in the attic. Suddenly the memories of that day—Tuesday, December 5, 1944, the eve of St. Nicolas Day—swelled in Brookins' mind, as vivid as if they had happened only a week ago.

"Mister Brookins are you still there?" Mueller asked, his voice once again breaking the silence.

"Uh…yes I am," a stunned and bewildered Brookins answered.

"You are the same person, yes? The one who was Saint Nicolas in Wiltz?"

"Yes…that was me. But I don't…"

"Wonderful! It is an honor to speak with you sir," Mueller exclaimed.

"An 'honor'?" Brookins said humbly. "Well…thank you. I'm…I'm sorry, what did you say your name was?"

"Yes…my name is Karl Mueller, and I am from Wiltz and I am calling to ask if you would help us to celebrate our anniversary…it has been thirty years."

"I'm sorry, I'm afraid I don't understand."

"It is the anniversary of the rebuilding of Wiltz. It has been thirty years and it would be a great honor if you would be a part of it," Mueller explained.

"Me?" asked the stunned Brookins.

"Yes, you…and your family. We would like to invite you to Luxembourg…to Wiltz…to be our guests for the celebration. It is in December."

"In December?" Brookins questioned, as he quickly added the numbers in his head. "Wait…that can't be right. The war didn't end until May in forty-five," he politely corrected. "That would make…let's see…it would be thirty-two years since the war ended…in May," Brookins stressed.

"No, no…," Mueller insisted. "I am sorry. Perhaps I did not fully explain. Please forgive me. This year…it is now thirty years from when we rebuilt Wiltz after the war. It is very special and we will celebrate in December on Saint Nicolas Day. And it would be an honor to have the very first American Saint Nicolas there."

"Oh I see," Brookins said, remembering the importance of the St. Nicolas tradition to the people of Luxembourg. "So you're going to celebrate the thirtieth anniversary of the rebuilding on this coming Saint Nicolas Day in December."

"Yes, that's correct," Mueller acknowledged.

"Well I'm honored…not to mention surprised, that you're inviting me…and my family…but I'm afraid…" Brookins stopped abruptly as something that Mueller had said suddenly struck him. "Hold on a second! What did you mean when you said the *first American Saint Nicolas*?"

"Yes of course! You are the very first American Saint Nicolas and it would be a great honor for you to come back."

"Yes, I got all that," Brookins said. "But what do you mean by *the first*," he asked. Of all the questions that were gathering in the back of his mind, this one was foremost.

Mueller fell silent for a moment, until he realized why there was such confusion.

"Ah…I see, Mister Brookins. Let me explain. After the war, the town…it was destroyed from all the bombs. We had to rebuild, but the people here in Wiltz always remembered the Americans and what they did, their…" Mueller paused as he tried to think of the English word, "…their sacrifices. We will *always* remember, just as we will always remember what you and the others did for the children on St. Nicolas Day. You brought Saint Nicolas Day back to life for the children." Mueller explained. "When Wiltz was reborn, we began a tradition to remember the American St. Nicolas and what he…what *you* did. Every year to honor you and the others, we have someone be the American Saint Nicolas. It is quite an honor to be chosen," Mueller emphasized. "That person goes through the town, just as you did, and they greet the children and give presents. Then we go to the castle for a celebration, just as you did. Last year I was the American Saint Nicolas. This year, on the thirty year anniversary of the rebuilding…well what a great honor it would be to have you, the *real* American Saint Nicolas, once again come to Wiltz."

Brookins sat on the bed speechless for a few moments, trying to absorb everything Karl Mueller had just said. All the questions Brookins had planned to ask were now gone from his mind.

"You see," Mueller continued, "all of Luxembourg celebrates Saint Nicolas Day, but here in Wiltz we also celebrate and remember you, the *American* Saint Nicolas. There is even a committee, 'Oeuvre Saint Nicolas'. We have been in charge of the celebration since 1949, you see. Please…it would be an honor if you would come to Wiltz for the anniversary. There will be many people from all over…many people."

"Well," Brookins said, "this is all quite a surprise. I suppose I, or rather we could come to Wiltz, but I'll have to talk it over with my family."

"Yes, yes…of course. Please let me give you my phone number and address so that you may contact me," Mueller said.

Brookins jotted down the information on the notepad next to the phone.

"Ok, I think I have it. Let me think about all this and then I'll contact you. You have to realize that it's been a long time. I mean…I haven't thought about any of this since the war, you understand."

"Yes of course. As for me, I think about this all the time," Mueller said.

"You do?"

"Oh yes. You see during the war I was seventeen years old," Mueller began, "and I had to hide from the Germans until the Americans arrived. Then the Germans came again during the Battle of the Bulge, and I had to hide again so they would not make me fight with them, as a German soldier, you see?"

"Yes I had heard that the Germans were doing that," Brookins sympathized.

"When the war ended I made a promise never to forget the Americans and how they fought for us...so that is why we started the Oeuvre St. Nicolas...to always remember."

"Yes, well I am honored," Brookins said, "and I will think about what you said."

"Yes...please, it would be a great honor."

"By the way, how did you get my phone number?" Brookins asked.

"We have Mister Frank McClelland to thank. He was the person who was able to find you. He too was with the American 28th Division. He was here in Wiltz a few weeks ago."

"I'm afraid I don't know who he is," said Brookins.

"You will meet him when you come to Wiltz," Mueller replied. "He too will be here for the anniversary, as our guest. Without him, we would not have found the American Saint Nicolas."

Brookins agreed to contact Mueller in a few days, and then hung up the phone. He sat on the edge of the bed, thinking about everything he'd just heard and about that one day in Wiltz in 1944. The memories and thoughts blended together and poured over him. No matter how many times he replayed the conversation, he just couldn't believe what Karl Mueller had told him. After sitting lost in thought for almost twenty minutes, Brookins finally got up and walked to the hallway. He pulled at a piece of rope hanging from a trap door in the ceiling, opening a set of folding stairs to the attic. He climbed up until he could reach the piece of string attached to the light, and gave it a tug. Instantly the bare bulb spilled its light onto the clutter of the attic. Brookins looked over to the far wall and spotted a dusty green trunk that had been tucked away in the corner of both the attic and his mind for years. He climbed the rest of the stairs and crouching below the rafters, made his way to the trunk. Inside were his old army clothes, and on top sat a piece of yellowed newspaper pressed between two pieces of clear plastic wrap. Brookins lifted the paper and tilted it towards the attic light. His eyes poured over the well-faded newspaper photo showing a young man in priest's robes riding in an army Jeep. He remembered coming home after the war and his mother telling him about that picture, the one that was seen in newspapers all across the country. She told him about the hundreds of cards and letters she had received from mothers who had seen that picture in their local newspapers and whose sons were also fighting in the war. They told her how lucky she was to know her son was alive and well and bringing so much joy to the poor children in Wiltz.

Brookins closed the lid of the trunk and climbed back down from the attic, the yellowed newspaper article still clutched in his hand. He walked back over to the phone and picked up the handset as he began dialing. Brookins gazed at the picture in the newspaper as he listened to the ringing on the other end of the phone.

"Hello," answered a weak and groggy voice.

"Oh geez...I didn't even realize the time!" Brookins remarked.

"Who is this?"

"It's Dick...Dick Brookins."

"Dick! Is everything all right?"

"Yes I'm fine. I'm sorry I woke you, I completely forgot about the time difference between here and the west coast."

"That's ok, how is everything?" the man on the other end of the phone asked after clearing his throat.

"Good...everything's good."

"It's been a long time."

"Yes it has...too long," Brookins agreed. "Listen Harry, you're not going to believe this...."

Richard Brookins' return to Wiltz began at the small Rochester, N.Y. airport. Though he usually had no trouble sleeping on airplanes, especially on long flights, Brookins now found it difficult to do anything but gaze out the window and think about Wiltz. With eleven hours of planes and airports ahead of him, he had plenty of time.

It had been four children, one grandchild, four promotions, two houses, four mortgages, eight cars, two dogs and a lifetime since he had last seen or even thought of the sleepy little town nestled in the Luxembourg countryside. In fact, the last time he had been in Wiltz was the day the Germans attacked the town at the beginning of the Battle of the Bulge.

Brookins stared out at the wispy clouds floating far beyond the jet's wingtip. In the attic of his mind, he opened the dusty footlocker where he'd stored away his memories of Wiltz and the war. He thought about the Christmas party and the happy faces of the children. He thought about the GIs who had given from their hearts and made the day special for the children. He also recalled the scramble to get out of Clervaux ahead of the attacking Germans and the hours of walking in the cold as he and Hugh Strauss had tried to get back to Wiltz. He wondered about the German soldiers he had to shoot…still hoping in his heart that they had made it. He thought about the ambulance that had offered to take him and Hugh to Wiltz, but only if they left their only weapon behind, and the laundry truck that finally got them back to town on a pile of clean clothes.

As the muffled rumbling of the jet engines droned on, Brookins continued to summon long forgotten memories of the turmoil he and Strauss encountered upon their return to Wiltz. The Germans were coming fast and despite the courageous efforts of the forward companies, it was obvious that the 28th Division was spread too thin to stop the German assault. After three days of fighting in the surrounding hills, the Division had no choice but to abandon its headquarters, and fall back. For Richard Brookins and the other soldiers in the Keystone Division, December 19, 1944, had been a sad and painful day.

When Brookins and his family stepped off the plane in Luxembourg City they were greeted by Karl Mueller and three other members of the Oeuvre St. Nicolas. Brookins had only spoken to Karl a few times and he didn't know any of the other men, yet he was welcomed as if they had known him all their lives...as if he were some distant cousin or uncle finally returning home after being away for years. In a way, these men *had* known Brookins all their lives, if only from the museum pictures and the story that had been passed down over the years.

The members of the Oeuvre St. Nicolas drove the Brookins family to Wiltz. Along the way, Brookins stared out at the rolling hills of the Ardennes and tried to catch a glimpse of something he might recognize. Aside from the countless pine trees and hardwoods that stretched skyward, Brookins saw nothing except the occasional roadside monument or plaque dedicated to the soldiers who fought and died on nearby battlefields. Such tributes now dotted the countryside honoring those who gave their lives to secure freedom for the people of Luxembourg.

Brookins and his family were taken to the Hotel Du Commerce, where they stayed for the week, and where a reception and dinner were planned in Brookins' honor the night before the big celebration.

Throughout the week, Brookins spent his days getting reacquainted with the town he'd know for only a few weeks in 1944. Everywhere he went people from the town would stop to meet him and shake his hand. Many of those who greeted him spoke some English; others spoke only German, French or Lëtzebuergesch; but regardless of the language, they all knew how to say "American Saint Nicolas."

On the day of the reception, Brookins made it a point to visit several places in and around Wiltz. His first stop took him to the Wiltz Castle and the museum. He took his time looking at the displays that portrayed major events of the war years. There were photos and artifacts from major battles, as well as displays honoring the people of Wiltz who organized the General Strike. The museum also included photographs detailing the events of December 5, 1944, when the American St. Nicolas arrived in Wiltz.

Brookins spent a good amount of time reading the captions and staring at the pictures. He remembered what had happened that day, but he could not remember anyone taking pictures. The evidence was neatly arranged on the wall in black and white photographs, but no matter how he tried to peer through the mist of time, he could not recall seeing anyone with a camera.

As the photos sparked more memories, he chuckled over how nervous he had been riding in the Jeep and meeting the children. He recalled being afraid that if he made a mistake, the people would never forgive him. As he studied the display, he remembered wearing the bishop's miter and how tight it had been. He remembered all these details, but he just could not remember seeing a camera.

After his stop at the Castle, Brookins and Frank McClelland, who had arrived a day after Brookins, visited a large stone memorial dedicated to the soldiers of the 28th Infantry. As relatives, townspeople, local military personnel and members of the press looked on, Brookins and McClelland placed a large wreath at the base of the memorial. The wreath was a solid circle, three feet in diameter and made entirely of roses: white on the outside, with red roses arranged in the shape of the 28th Division's keystone shoulder patch in the center. After placing the wreath, Brookins and McClelland took a few steps back and paused to remember their fellow soldiers, many of whom never made it out of Wiltz.

Brookins' final stop before the reception was the American Military Cemetery in Hamm, just outside of Luxembourg City. More than five thousand American soldiers were buried there, in razor-straight rows that radiated out from a central monument, a white stone cross or Star of David marking each neatly manicured grave. Many of the men were victims of the fighting during the Battle of the Bulge. At one end of the massive field lay the grave of General George S. Patton, whose U.S. Third Army had been headquartered in Luxemburg City and who had died shortly after the war.

Brookins walked among the graves, reading the names of the soldiers, until he came across one more memory...the grave of Edgar Stine. Eddie was another of Brookins' friends who stayed behind in Wiltz; one who never made it out. Tears welled up in Brookins' eyes as he read Eddie's name chiseled into the stone cross.

"We won, Eddie...we won," Brookins said softly. He bent down to place some flowers on Eddie's grave. He wiped the tears from his eyes, and after a few minutes of remembering his good friend, turned and walked away.

By the time Brookins arrived back at the hotel, he had put away the sorrow and pain of the day's visits, choosing instead to think about the reception that night and the St. Nicolas ceremonies the next day.

The dining hall of the Hotel Du Commerce was filled to capacity that evening with dignitaries, local clergy and school teachers, representatives from the US Ambassador's office, and some of the townspeople who were there the first time Brookins played St. Nicolas. There was also a camera crew on hand to film the entire event for NBC news.

The room erupted with cheers and applause as Brookins and his wife and family stepped into the room. A bit unnerved by the attention, Brookins smiled awkwardly and waved to the crowd. As he glanced around the room, his attention was drawn to a corner where he spotted a small man with a round face, wide smile and bright eyes. Brookins hurried over to embrace him.

"You son-of-a-bitch, I knew you'd make it," Brookins said, his voice cracking with emotion.

"I wouldn't have missed this for the world," Harry Stutz answered. "I would have been here sooner but the weather in Chicago was a mess. They kept delaying my flight out. I just got in this afternoon."

"It's been crazy here too. People have been coming up to me since I got here; shaking my hand, hugging me, and showing me pictures from the war. It's amazing. I had no idea this was such a big thing."

"I guess they never forgot about us, eh?"

"You can say that again. You know, Harry, this is all because of you, really."

"Well, we were all involved, remember?"

"Yes, I know, but all this…this attention, the ceremonies, this whole Saint Nicolas thing is because of you…it was all your idea. You're the one who should be getting all this attention, not me."

"Well you seem to be doing a fine job for all of us," Harry grinned.

Brookins smiled. "Well in that case, I should get over to the head table…but we've got a lot of catching up to do later."

"I'll be here," Harry said, "Now go on Saint Nick…do your thing."

Following dinner, several members of the Oeuvre St. Nicolas delivered tributes to Brookins, Stutz, McClelland and the other men of the 28th Infantry. Then it was time for everyone to mingle and meet the American St. Nicolas. One by one everyone in the room stepped up to meet Brookins. They would shake his hand and tell him what an honor it was to meet him, and Brookins would politely listen to their stories and recollections; what the American St. Nicolas meant to them and their children; or how they never forgot what he and the other soldiers did for them throughout the war.

After most of the people had met and talked with Brookins, a member of the NBC camera crew asked if they could have a few minutes to interview him. Brookins, who by now was reveling in the festivities, was more than happy to accommodate, but as he followed the reporter over to where the crew had set up the lights and camera, a man and two middle-aged women stopped him.

"Excuse me, Mister Brookins," the man began. "These women would like to meet you, but they do not speak English."

"Certainly," Brookins said smiling at the already beaming women.

"I can interpret for them," the man added.

One of the women spoke in French, and as the interpreter listened carefully Brookins smiled and nodded, awaiting the translation.

"She says you probably do not remember her or her sister," the man related.

"I'm sorry I don't," Brookins said. "Were you here in 1944?"

The interpreter thought for a moment, and then spoke to the women. The two women looked at each other with surprise and laughed. The second woman spoke to the translator, but before the man could respond, Brookins had pieced together bits of the conversation and a look of surprise spread across his face.

"My angels!" he blurted out with a smile.

No translation was necessary as Brookins and the two women, Greta and Anna Shultzmann, exchanged hugs and kisses and tears.

"These were my angels," Brookins said to the interpreter. "I can't believe it! It's so good to see you again," he said hugging them both.

"I remember," Anna recalled through the interpreter, "The word went around town that the Americans were collecting all their rations to give a party for the children. Then the Mother Superior came into our class to tell us about the party and that two of us would be chosen to be St. Nicolas' angels."

"Yes, it was such an honor to be chosen," Greta said. "I remember you lifting us into the Jeep and we drove through the whole town. Then we went back to the castle for the party."

"Yes and there was hot cocoa," Anna continued through the interpreter. "And everyone sang songs. It was such a wonderful day. Then when we were ready to go home, Saint Nicolas came over to us angels and gave each of us a kiss."

Brookins smiled as he recalled the moments the women were talking about.

"Well, I can remember that I tried to talk to you both all day and you didn't say a word. I'm glad you decided to talk to me now," he joked. "I don't suppose you'd want to be my angels again tomorrow?" he teased.

The women laughed after they heard the translation, and shook their heads.

The thought occurred to Brookins that, like the other children in 1944, Anna and Greta had seen him not as a soldier, but as the real St. Nicolas. What a delight it must have been from a child's perspective, to be St. Nicolas' helpers and to have him treat them in such a special manner.

"I have to go over there to talk to the camera crew," Brookins explained to the women. "Will you wait here until I'm done?"

The women nodded and once more the three of them exchanged hugs. Then Brookins walked over to where the camera crew had set up the lights.

"I know you want to get back to the festivities, so we'll make this as quick as possible," the crew's producer promised as Brookins sat down.

"That's all right," Brookins said as a technician placed a microphone in front of him, "Ask whatever you want...I'm just happy to be here for all of this."

"Let's get started then," the producer said.

As the camera rolled, the producer asked Brookins to describe what it was like the day the Germans retook the town of Wiltz. Brookins thought for a moment and then explained how the attack had caught the Americans by surprise and how he and the other soldiers felt ashamed at being forced to retreat and abandon the people they had come to know so well. To make matters worse, the men had learned that some of the people at the party had been killed and the town of Wiltz destroyed in the fighting that followed the assault.

The producer nodded and asked Brookins if part of the reason he came back was to make amends with the people of Wiltz. After thinking about the question for a moment, Brookins shook his head and explained that he wanted to come back to Wiltz because he felt grateful to the people. They had such tremendous loyalty to American veterans and America in general after all that had happened during the war. He added that he felt proud because in some small way he represented all the men who had helped with the Christmas party, especially those who couldn't be there because they'd lost their lives defending the town.

The cameraman interrupted the producer just as he was preparing to ask another question. "I'll need another reel," he said, quickly swapping out the film.

Brookins' thoughts drifted as he watched the man reload the film. He thought back to the many times he had swapped out reels of film while showing movies to the troops, but before his thoughts could take him too far into the past, the cameraman was ready again.

The producer asked Brookins about the party and what it was like to play Saint Nicolas in 1944. Then he asked if Brookins had been surprised to learn of the town's annual reenactment.

"I sure was!" Brookins exclaimed, "I had no idea that any of this was going on until several months ago when I got a call from the St. Nicolas Day Committee. You have to remember that it was just one day out of the whole war. Don't get me wrong, it was a wonderful day and we all…that is, the GIs and the kids and everyone…had a great time, but there was still a war going on. We had our jobs to do and we moved on. We never did come back to Wiltz after the Germans attacked. I had pretty much forgotten about Wiltz and the Christmas party. So when they called and asked me to come back, well, at first I didn't believe it, but now, after all this…," Brookins paused as the words began to catch in his throat, "I never knew it meant so much to the people here."

Richard Brookins, The American St. Nick, returns to Wiltz; December 1977
Courtesy of the Oeuvre St. Nicolas, Wiltz

The American St. Nick with his angels; December 1977
Courtesy of the Oeuvre St. Nicolas, Wiltz

The American St. Nicolas once again leads the procession through the streets of Wiltz; December 1977

Courtesy of the Oeuvre St. Nicolas, Wiltz

Harry Stutz (left) and Richard Brookins (2nd from right) making a presentation on behalf of the vetrans of the 28th Division, December 1977

Courtesy of the Private Collection of Richard Brookins

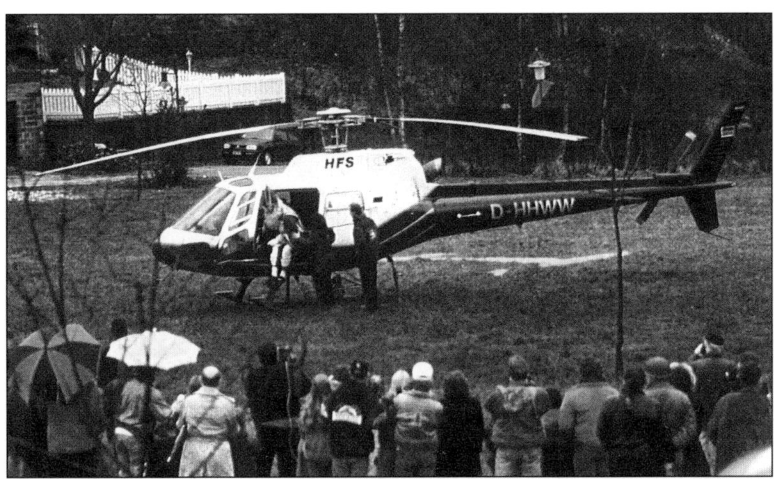

The American St. Nicolas arriving by helicopter in Wiltz; December 1994

Courtesy of the Oeuvre St. Nicolas, Wiltz

Memorial to the Men of the 28th Division at Wiltz, Luxembourg

Courtesy of the Oeuvre St. Nicolas, Wiltz

Richard Brookins returns for the 50th anniversary celebration of the American St. Nicolas in Wiltz; December 1999

Courtesy of the Oeuvre St. Nicolas, Wiltz

The American St. Nicolas along with his angels, riding his sleigh through Wiltz; December 1999

Courtesy of the Oeuvre St. Nicolas, Wiltz

The American St. Nicolas greeting the children and handing out presents; December 1999
Courtesy of the Oeuvre St. Nicolas, Wiltz

The American St. Nicolas on his throne; December 1999
Courtesy of the Oeuvre St. Nicolas, Wiltz

Joseph Steiner was a ten-year-old boy in Wiltz when he first met the American St. Nicolas in 1944. He, like most of the people in Wiltz, never forgot that day and the generosity of the American soldiers. It was an *event*, a Christmas story, passed down through the generations and retold countless times in homes throughout Wiltz and the surrounding towns. Now forty years old and a father himself, Steiner waited in the cold with his two children and more than three thousand other people to see the American St. Nicolas once again arrive in Wiltz.

Off in the distance of a clear December sky, the small crowd that had gathered on the outskirts of town could see a helicopter approaching. It was Karl Mueller's idea to make the arrival of the American

St. Nicolas, on this 30th Anniversary a special one. He contacted the nearby U.S. Army base and persuaded them to join the festivities by flying Brookins into town in one of their helicopters. As the helicopter approached, the rumbling of the engine and the high-pitched thump of the blades grew louder, as did the excitement of the onlookers. They watched as the aircraft gracefully eased its way down from the sky and landed in the middle of an open field. The pilot cut the engine and as the rotor blades stopped turning, one of the doors in the passenger compartment opened. A loud ovation rose from the crowd and echoed through the hills as the unmistakable figure of a man dressed in a gold trimmed cape, and a red bishop's miter, with a puffy white beard and a crosier, emerged from the helicopter. For the first time in more than thirty years, *the* American St. Nicolas was back in Wiltz.

The mayor of Wiltz, members of the Oeuvre St. Nicolas, and Father Wolffe all greeted Brookins. They exchanged handshakes and Brookins was ushered over to a parade float built just for the occasion. On the horse-drawn float stood an ornate sleigh adorned with shimmering garlands and flanked on either side by two little girls dressed as angels. Brookins stepped onto the platform and to the delight of the crowd, started waving. This time, Brookins was well aware of the camera crew filming the event. He waved to the camera and then nodded to the man holding the reigns of the horse team. The man gave the reigns a tug and the float slowly moved forward.

The narrow streets of the town were lined with more people eager to catch a glimpse of the American St. Nicolas as he made his way to Wiltz Castle and the official ceremony. The route through town was exactly the same as it had been more than thirty years earlier. As the float journeyed through the streets, Brookins waved to the spectators and tried to make eye contact with as many of the children as possible.

"Merry Christmas," he repeated over and over again as he passed out candy to the children, this time tossing it to them from the sleigh.

The ride through town took a bit longer than the Oeuvre St. Nicolas had planned, but after thirty minutes, the float finally glided up to the Castle's amphitheater, followed by a procession of people from the streets. An anxious crowd waiting at the amphitheater erupted in joyous cheers at the sight of the American St. Nicolas. An amazed Brookins waved to the crowd for a few moments before stepping down from the float. While a band played and the crowd sang songs in praise of St. Nicolas, Brookins strode up onto the stage where a group of dignitaries, including Harry Stutz and Frank McClelland, were waiting. When the songs ended and the subsequent applause subsided, Karl Mueller walked up to the microphone and addressed the crowd in English.

"What a wonderful day it is here in Wiltz, to have *the* American Saint Nicolas, the very first, Mister Richard Brookins, here with us to celebrate," Mueller said proudly, and then paused as the amphitheater once again erupted in applause and cheers.

"We can never forget what these American soldiers did for us, and especially for our children."

Mueller paused again as the crowd punctuated his remarks with applause.

"Now, let me introduce Father Wolffe for the blessing."

Father Wolffe was already on his way up to the podium. The priest was older, rounder and slower than the last time Brookins had seen him, but his eyes were still bright and focused, and his memory sharp. He arrived at the podium just as the applause began to subside. He adjusted the microphone, nervously cleared his throat a couple of times and began reading in English.

"If Luxembourg would stand another thousand years," he began, "we would always be grateful to the Americans and their most brave and valiant nation."

Another ovation rose from the audience and continued for almost a minute until the priest finally raised his hands to quiet the crowd.

"May God bless you all and keep you well this Saint Nicolas Day," Father Wolffe said as he gestured the sign of the cross first to the left, then the middle, then to the right side of the hushed amphitheater. After clearing his throat one more time, he turned back to the microphone.

"It is my pleasure and honor to introduce Mister Richard Brookins...the American Saint Nicolas."

Everyone in the amphitheater stood, cheering and applauding loudly as the American St. Nicolas made his way to the podium. Brookins hadn't been nervous about reenacting his role as St. Nicolas; not when the helicopter approached the landing field and he could see more than a hundred people waiting for his arrival; not when the NBC camera crew began filming and he knew there was a better than average chance that the images caught on film would be seen all over Europe and maybe even in the United States; and not even when the float made its way into the Castle courtyard to the delight of more than three thousand people. It wasn't until Brookins began the short walk to the podium that he felt his stomach tighten and his breath quicken. The same anxiety he had felt stepping out of the Jeep in 1944 seized him again as he reached the podium and waved to the crowd. He glanced behind him, scanning the faces on the stage until he saw Harry Stutz, who smiled and nodded encouragingly, just as he had thirty years ago. Brookins took a deep breath, and turned back to the crowd, ready to deliver one last surprise for St. Nicolas Day.

He reached into his pocket and took out the notes he had rehearsed a hundred times over; then, with his hand trembling, he adjusted the microphone and began to speak.

The thousands of people gathered in the amphitheater fell silent with astonishment as the American St. Nicolas spoke to them, for the first time, in their own language.

Since 1977, Frank McClelland, Harry Stutz and Richard Brookins have each returned to Wiltz numerous times to visit life-long friends, and every year on the Sunday preceding December 6, the small storybook town holds its annual St. Nicolas Day celebration. Each year Richard Brookins is invited to recreate his role as the American St. Nicolas.

December 2004 marks the 60th anniversary of the American St. Nicolas in Wiltz.

Richard Brookins plans to be there.